Our Shared British Future
Muslims and Integration in the UK

The Muslim Council of Britain

Published in 2018 by the © Muslim Council of Britain.

Muslim Council of Britain, PO Box 57330, London, E1 2WJ, UK

admin@mcb.org.uk | @muslimcouncil | www.mcb.org.uk

The views expressed in this publication are those of the author(s), and do not necessarily reflect the views of the Muslim Council of Britain or its affiliates.

We appreciate the generous support provided by Muslim Aid and The Muslim Council of Britain Charitable Foundation towards the publication of this report.

ISBN: 978-1-905461-05-9

Contents

Foreword

I am delighted to showcase here a collection of diverse voices on integration in Britain today. They come from scholars, activists, specialists and leaders who all bring unique perspectives, expertise and life experiences to this issue.

Unfortunately, the debate on integration is skewed in one direction. It invariably involves Muslims and comes with the implicit accusation that Muslims are incapable of integrating into British society.

Of course, we would disagree. In fact, as our Islamic scholars in this publication state, our faith encourages us to actively engage in this plural society we share. However, many Muslims do face challenges in partaking fully in British life. Youth unemployment, poverty, discrimination and issues related to identity crises and belonging, are challenges that transcend communities.

If any integration policy is to succeed, as the government plans to do in 2018, it needs to be inclusive. The same goes for 'British values', a relatively new term coined after concerns of extremism. Many are worried that such values have been conceived in a knee-jerk fashion because some people are considered 'not quite British enough' and therefore must be subject to a civilising mission.

I am grateful for the many contributors to this publication, including Rt Hon Diane Abbott MP, Rt Hon Dominic Grieve QC MP and Baroness Warsi. Their views from Westminster will add to the understanding we are trying to build of integration and Muslims in the UK. I am also grateful to Muslim Aid for their sponsorship of this report and its launch in Parliament. Their UK programmes including The Big Food Drive in partnership with Crisis to feed the homeless and Interfaith Projects are models for our society.

HARUN KHAN

Harun Khan is the Secretary General of the Muslim Council of Britain. He was elected to the post in 2016.

Muslim Council of Britain

OVER 2 MILLION MUSLIMS

4.8% OF OVERALL POPULATION IN ENGLAND+WALES

1,409,290

1,296,776

TOTAL = 2,706,066

ETHNICALLY DIVERSE

Asian/Asian British
1,830,560

Black/African/Caribbean/Black British
272,015

White
210,620

Arab
178,195

Any Other Ethnic Group
112,094

Mixed/Multiple Ethnic Group
102,582

AGE PROFILE

33% AGED 15 OR UNDER

4% AGED 65+

8.1% OF ALL SCHOOL-AGE CHILDREN ARE MUSLIM

BRITISH BORN & BRED

 47.2% MUSLIMS BORN IN UK

ONLY **6%** MUSLIMS ARE STRUGGLING WITH SPEAKING ENGLISH

 **73%** OF MUSLIMS STATE THEIR ONLY NATIONAL IDENTITY IS BRITISH

26 PARLIAMENTARY CONSTITUENCIES HAVE A MUSLIM POPULATION OF 20% OR MORE

Muslims in the UK

Taken from the report:
*British Muslims in Numbers:
A Demographic, Socio-economic and Health profile
of Muslims in Britain drawing
on the 2011 Census*

Access the report at:

www.mcb.org.uk/
muslimstatistics/

MUSLIMS AT WORK

20% ARE 'ECONOMICALLY ACTIVE' (FULL-TIME EMPLOYMENT)
(compared to 35% in overall population)

29% 16-24 YEAR OLD MUSLIM WOMEN IN EMPLOYMENT
(compared to approx 50% in overall population)

18% 16-74 YEAR OLD MUSLIM WOMEN 'LOOKING AFTER HOME OR FAMILY'
(compared to 6% in overall population)

5.5% OF MUSLIMS IN THE 'HIGHER MANAGERIAL, ADMINISTRATIVE + PROFESSIONAL OCCUPATIONS' CATEGORY

EDUCATION

329,694 MUSLIMS IN FULL-TIME EDUCATION

24% OF THE MUSLIM POPULATION (OF AGE 16 AND ABOVE) HAVE DEGREE LEVEL AND ABOVE QUALIFICATIONS

43% OF MUSLIM FULL-TIME STUDENTS ARE FEMALE

39% **2001**   **26%** **2011**
MUSLIMS WITH 'NO QUALIFICATIONS'

INTEGRATION AND MUSLIMS

Five key points policymakers should consider
when approaching integration strategies.

1 — ## EQUAL INTEGRATION FOR ALL

Recognise that integration must truly be a 'two-way street' with no specific or special onus on Muslim communities. This should be part of a vision for a nation that treats everyone as equal citizens.

2 — ## BREAK DOWN BARRIERS

Ensure steps are taken to tackle the real challenges to integration, faced by Muslim communities and as identified by Muslim communities.

3 — ## CELEBRATE BRITISH DIVERSITY

Understand the diversity of Muslim communities and celebrate the successes of our integration model.

4 — ## FAITH AIDS INTEGRATION

Religiosity is not a barrier to integration. It helps communities come together. The media debate unfairly casts suspicion on Muslims who practice their faith.

5 — ## DO NOT CONFLATE EXTREMISM WITH INTEGRATION

Integration strategies are hampered if seen through the prism of security.

Building Our Two-Way Street

'Integration is a two-way street': those were the famous words of former Prime Minister David Cameron just over 10 years ago after staying with a Muslim family.

It is perhaps one of the best expressions of what 'Britishness' is all about; simple and inclusive, it articulated a vision where we all had a part to play without singling out any one group for special treatment or special opprobrium.

Integration is a laudable policy objective. Yet too often we see the conception of a 'top-down, mono-nationalist and establishment 'British values' approach'[1] which assumes the 'other' needs to be civilised into our way of thinking, and in essence puts the 'moral onus on ethnic minorities for the supposed failures of integration.'[2]

Such an approach betrays not only a refusal to fully understand our challenges but also flies in the face of the pragmatic reality that we are a nation of immigrants, demonstrated all too clearly recently with the revelation that the first modern Briton – Cheddar Man – had 'dark to black' skin.

This 'two-way street' approach apportions responsibilities on all of our society to aspire to universal values of democracy, the rule of law, individual liberty, mutual respect and tolerance of those of different faiths and beliefs.

Integration for us means integration for everyone. Since the former Prime Minister articulated his two-way street metaphor, the path has narrowed with traffic expected to come from one way only. This stems from a moral panic that has generated in the last decade primarily around Muslims. It is one where Muslims are the victims of a culture war not of their own choosing.

So, when Muslims embrace the value of democracy by entering public life, too often their motives are questioned and they are accused of 'entryism'.[3] Or take the other value of the rule of law, which when some Muslims uphold, becomes 'lawfare'.[4] Individual liberty, too, cannot be foregone because a public does not like the clothing choices made by a small minority of Muslims,[5] while mutual respect excludes Muslims when over 30% of young children think Muslims are taking over England.

The academic Tariq Modood's words frame the discussion of integration powerfully:

> 'we have to understand that there are different modes of integration and none of them – including multiculturalism – is to be dismissed. Because in a multicultural society different groups will integrate in different ways. Some ethnic minorities may wish to assimilate, some to have the equal rights of integrated citizens, some to maintain the cultural differences of their group identities, and some to be free to choose cosmopolitan mixed identities. Equally, the majority society may look on different minority groups in all these different ways. Each approach has a particular conception of equal citizenship but the value of each can only be realised if it is not imposed but is the preferred choice of minority individuals and groups. No singular model is likely to be suitable for all groups. To have a reasonable chance of integrating the maximum number of members of minorities, none of these political responses should be dismissed.'[6]

When it comes to integration, the British Muslim story is positive but still challenging. There are over 2 million Muslims in this country. 33% are aged 15 and under, 47% were born in this country. Only 6% of Muslims are struggling to speak English and 73% are proud to state that their national identity is British.

The current anxieties around integration – expressed implicitly and explicitly – include the myth that many Muslims do not or are not capable of integrating because of the supposed strictures of their faith. The grassroots reality, however, is very different. In actual fact we have a lot to celebrate: a growing proportion (89% in 2015-2016) thought 'their local area is a place where people from different backgrounds get on well,'[7] and despite claims to the contrary, Muslim communities have become less segregated according to the latest Census.[8] When looking at the challenges of the rise of the far-right in many parts of Europe, and of Trumpism in the United States of America, we have a lot to be thankful for.

However, the expectation that an immigrant must show 'gratitude to the country that offered his mother and him so much,'[9] is a xenophobic attitude that undermines the equality that all citizens should be afforded.

In the Muslim Council of Britain submission to the Casey Review, we highlighted that a 'culture of fear is emerging which is a big driver in preventing a more united and cohesive society.' We said: 'We must recognise that our public discourse and conversation has a part to play in furthering integration. Integration is fostered when the media reports on stories that speak of achievement of minorities, of people coming together and where national moments are shared by all.'

The good, the bad, the normal – all Muslims in their full diversity – cannot and should not be treated as anything but equal citizens, and our expectations cannot be different.

In that light and with that positive vision of an equal society, this report platforms voices from a range of diverse backgrounds and perspectives on integration relevant to Muslim communities.

When it comes to integration, the British Muslim story is positive but still challenging.

Whilst this report commissioned by the Muslim Council of Britain rightly focusses on Muslim communities, any national integration strategy should have a broader outlook. Care should be taken to recognise the dangers of encompassing integration under the banner of extremism, and falsehoods about immigration – issues covered in the first section of the report.

A national integration strategy must also avoid the London-centricity that permeates many reports. Section two brings to the fore views from integration stories across the UK including Northern Ireland, Scotland, Wales, Bradford, Blackburn, Birmingham and London.

The understanding of the role of Muslims in our national history and our nation today, is pivotal for the wider society. This – covered in section four – includes the impact of colonisation, Muslims' contribution to the World War I and how the diversity of Muslims make up "Al-Britannia".

Section five then dives deeper into the diversity of Muslim experiences, including the views of converts, students, young people, Muslim women and Muslims from South London's Nigerian communities.

Finally, the report hears from scholars on how our faith informs our life in a plural society, how to best relate to others and how to be an embodiment of our values by speaking out against injustice.

Rather than repeating arguments made ad nauseam by detractors of Muslim communities, this report seeks to reframe the discussion from the perspective of under-represented voices, and to inform to the national conversation on integration.

MIQDAAD VERSI

Miqdaad Versi is Assistant Secretary General of the Muslim Council of Britain. He is most renowned for his work tackling media misreporting, having elicited over 50 corrections from national press and was named by the BBC as "The man correcting stories on Muslims".

Notes

1. Who speaks to England: Labour's English Challenge, Tariq Modood in The Fabian Society, November 2016

2. The Casey Review is an ill-conceived intervention, Oliver Kamm in Prospect Magazine, December 2016

3. Counter-Extremism Strategy, HM Government, October 2015

4. William Shawcross is right: Islamists are skilled at lawfare, Douglas Murray in The Spectator, October 2015

5. Conservative MP Philip Hollobone refuses to meet with constituents wearing a veil, Daily Telegraph, July 2010

6. Multiculturalism and the Nation, Tariq Modood in Labour List, November 2012

7. Community Life Survey 2015-16 Statistical Bulletin, Cabinet Office, July 2016

8. Dynamics of Diversity: Evidence from the 2011 Census- More segregation or more mixing, Ludi Simpson in Centre of Dynamics of Ethnicity, December 2012

9. Platell's people: Can't you show a scintilla of gratitude Stormzy, Amanda Platetll in the Daily Mail, February 2018

Views from Westminster

RT HON DIANE ABBOTT MP

My vision is a Britain that celebrates the profound and enriching transformation brought about by diversity and multiculturalism. Individuals, who, with all their different experiences, talents and contributions make for a fairer and more equal nation, where no-one is held back. A Britain that is free from every form of racism, anti-Semitism, Islamophobia and discrimination.

Our approach to integration is to work together with communities to break down the barriers that hold us back from this aspiration.

We must understand the real challenges faced across our communities, and support each other, rather than demonise those communities.

We must stand up to those who wish to stir division and look to break up our communities, by spreading fear and hatred of the 'other'.

We must not merely tolerate difference and diversity, but respect and celebrate its impact on our nation.

That is why I am so pleased to support the work of the Muslim Council of Britain and the deep and longstanding positive impact Muslim communities have made in our country.

The next Labour government will ensure a Britain that works for the many, not the few.

RT HON DIANE ABBOTT MP

Rt Hon Diane Abbott MP represents the constitutency for Hackney North and Stoke Newington and is Shadow Secretary of State for Home Affairs. In 1987 Diane Abbott made history by becoming the first black woman ever elected to the British Parliament.

RT HON DOMINIC GRIEVE QC MP

My work as Chair of the Citizens UK inquiry into Muslim participation in public life has left me optimistic about our country's future. We may have identified problems but we saw how beneficial change is occurring as well. A younger generation of Muslims comfortable with their religious, national and local identities are making a positive contribution to the wellbeing of their neighbourhoods by working with all to achieve shared goals.

I am convinced these examples can be built upon. But doing so also requires addressing those areas where lack of interaction with others creates isolation and misunderstanding. If we do, our entire society will reap great benefits for the future.

RT HON DOMINIC GRIEVE QC MP

Rt Hon Dominic Grieve QC MP represents the constituency of Beaconsfield and has served in the Cabinet as Attorney General and Justice Secretary. He is currently chair of the Intelligence and Security Committee of Parliament.

BARONESS SAYEEDA WARSI

The debate on integration has too often been based on ideology not evidence.

A community is best integrated when it feels it belongs and matters. As long as economic, social and political barriers prevent individuals in our nation achieving their full potential, they will neither belong nor matter. As long as the narrative from some sectors of officialdom and sections of the press continues to define Muslims as the "other", the process of integration becomes more challenging.

For nearly a decade I have been calling on politicians across the political landscape to engage widely and deeply with all communities that make up Britain. Sadly, when it comes to British Muslims, the policy of disengagement applied by successive governments has led to more and more British Muslim individuals and groups viewed as 'beyond the pale' and thus pushed out of the mainstream and into the margins.

I have heard numerous accounts of how a community distrusted has struggled to engage and play its full part in all aspects of our nations life.

Unpicking some of the myths around this debate is a constructive and important contribution to creating a sense of ease amongst all that make up our shared home.

BARONESS SAYEEDA WARSI

Baroness Sayeeda Warsi was the first British Muslim woman to serve in Cabinet, as Minister for Foreign Affairs, for Communities and as Co-Chair of the Conservative Party. Her book *The Enemy Within: A Tale of Muslim Britain* was published in 2017.

Section One
Dealing With Integration Myths

Integration is Not About Extremism

The debate on integration, immigration and the system of core values which should unite all citizens of our country has been poisoned by the impact of violent extremism in all its forms. Extremists want to sow division; they abhor the fact that people of so many different faiths and ethnic backgrounds live side by side in our communities.

I have been very fortunate. My parents came to the UK from Ireland in the fifties and I find it amazing that in one generation their son can become Chief Constable of Greater Manchester and knighted by Her Majesty. It says something about the opportunities offered to immigrants who come to this country. On the other hand, growing up in East London I was conscious that as Irish Catholics we were different and there are aspects of English culture and tradition I still don't fully understand because they were not part of my upbringing.

In my police career I was fortunate to serve in a number of ethnically diverse communities in the West Midlands and Greater Manchester. I took on national police responsibility for the Prevent Programme. I have been to many welcoming community events and celebrations but at the same time shared in the pain at Holocaust memorial services or other occasions when I have experienced the profound hurt caused by hatred and prejudice. I have had many difficult conversations with members of the Muslim faith about Prevent but it has always been in an atmosphere of mutual respect and the privilege of getting to understand the richness of the Muslim faith.

I am not sure what integration is and whether I think it is a good thing. Some commentators say that multiculturalism in the UK model has failed. I profoundly disagree. The model of allowing people from different traditions and ethnic backgrounds to follow their traditions, but under the rule of our law, democratic principles and respect for fundamental human rights, is an example to the rest of the world. Of course, we have had our challenges especially with the profound impact of young people from our country carrying out violent terrorist attacks against others, but it is bizarre to blame this on multiculturalism.

> *We have had our challenges especially with the profound impact of young people from our country carrying out violent terrorist attacks... but it is bizarre to blame this on multiculturalism.*

You cannot force integration. The French have tried this through fining women for wearing the hijab and discouraging all forms of ethnic monitoring. The approach seems to have merely created a profound alienation among their minority communities and certainly has not prevented a series of very violent attacks in recent years. Attempts by the UK Government to promote 'British values' was unsuccessful; this was not surprising when one of the most profound British values is arguably 'live and let live.'

One of the most challenging times during my tenure as Chief Constable was just after the *Charlie Hebdo* terrorist attacks in Paris. The first reaction was to show solidarity with the French police officers who had been killed. Every police force in the UK held a remembrance event in order to send the pictures to the families of our deceased French colleagues. But the attacks had an impact beyond the police. Members of the Manchester Jewish community spoke to me and said they were scared, they feared a backlash and they were not sure they had a future in this country. They wanted more armed patrols. Members of the Muslim community spoke to me and said they too felt scared, they feared a backlash and were not sure they had a future in this country. They also wanted more patrols. It struck me that there could be another approach; one which would not allow the terrorists to sow division, but where the different communities stood together.

The campaign we started #WeStandTogether was adopted nationally and has been featured by the Football Association at Wembley. It brought together people from all different backgrounds in Manchester. It was not about trying to force people to be the same, but rather that our common humanity and decency, our respect for life which unites us all, is far stronger than what divides us. We encouraged local community events which brought different groups together, celebrated the different festivals together and opened up places of worship for others to visit. This is not about downplaying difference however, and #WeStandTogether is just as much about creating safe places where difficult conversations can be had about the things that divide us, but in an atmosphere of mutual respect.

The effort by so many remarkable people came to fruition after the horrendous attack at the Manchester Arena when the immediate reaction of the people of Manchester was not to be afraid, not to turn against one another, but to stand together in unity against hatred and violence.

So, I am not a great fan of integration — it sounds too much like forcing everyone to think and act the same. I prefer cohesion which recognises the enormous richness of diversity built on a common set of values. It cannot be imposed from the national level; it has to be built from the bottom up by ordinary folk making the effort to understand their own prejudice, and making the effort to reach out to whoever they regard as 'the stranger'.

Young people get this. Whatever may be the national picture or the impact of terrorism, they look beyond the label to see the real person underneath. You see it every day in the groups of students going to and from school in their friendship groups, apparently blind to the ethnic distinctions that my own generation were obsessed with.

So, let us not focus on confronting extremism. Let us focus on promoting diversity and cohesion, creating safe spaces for honest discussion about our fears and prejudices and our concerns about the practices and beliefs of other cultures. Let us call out the haters to debate openly and expose their attitudes to the spotlight of logic, and recognise you build cohesion brick by brick through individual acts of tolerance, courtesy, friendship and looking beyond that label for the human beneath. #WeStandTogether

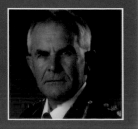

SIR PETER FAHY

Sir Peter Fahy is a retired senior British police officer. He was the Chief Constable of Greater Manchester Police, the United Kingdom's third largest police force, and former National Policing Lead of Prevent.

Immigrants Make Us Prosperous

1. Jobs and wages

Do immigrants take jobs away from existing residents? Not necessarily – economists call this the 'lump of labour fallacy' , the idea that there's only a fixed number of jobs. Immigrants do take jobs, but because they earn money and spend it, adding to demand in the economy, they also indirectly create new jobs.

Over time, this is likely to balance out – and that's what seems to happen in the UK. It's very hard indeed to argue that immigration increases unemployment, when unemployment in the UK is at a forty year low after a period of historically very high immigration. Moreover, when we look at the geography of unemployment, we find that overall areas with higher levels of immigration (historic or recent) don't have higher levels of unemployment, suggesting that any negative impacts are small or zero. Nor is there any evidence that immigration has impacted the employment prospects of specific groups such as the young or unskilled.

Similarly, there's not much evidence that immigration reduces wages overall, but it may have some, small, negative impact on low-skilled workers. The most recent analysis found that immigration since 2004 may have reduced wages for native workers in the low-skilled service sector by about 1%, or put another way would have depressed annual pay increases by about a penny an hour. The impact in other sectors is even smaller. So, while migration may have had some small negative impact on wages for the low paid, other factors, positive and negative (technological change, policies on tax credits, the National Minimum Wage) seem to have been far more important.

2. Growth and Productivity

The UK's recent performance on growth, and especially productivity, has been very poor. But this seems to coincide with the financial crisis and its aftermath (which of course in turn led to a fall in migration) rather than the earlier sharp rise in migration. Internationally, the evidence seems to suggest migration is good for productivity (and hence per capita GDP). This could be for a variety of reasons. High skilled migration could boost productivity directly, low skilled migration could increase the flexibility and responsiveness of the economy filling gaps, meaning native workers could be more productive. Or there may be a wider impact; diversity may make companies more productive, or migrants may be particularly likely to be entrepreneurial or innovative.

> *It's very hard indeed to argue that immigration increases unemployment, when unemployment in the UK is at a forty year low after a period of historically very high immigration.*

3. Impacts on taxes, spending and public services

Immigrants increase the demand for public services – schools, hospitals and so on – but they also pay taxes, which help to fund public services. Overall the balance is likely to be positive, particularly for recent migrants, since taxes come mostly from the working population. While much public spending is on the very young or the retired, it is hardly surprising that young migrants in employment make an initial positive fiscal contribution. However, this doesn't mean that immigration will not have an impact on demands on public services at a local level, especially if funding doesn't adjust to reflect new pressures. But broader worries seem to be unfounded. Areas with higher levels of immigration don't have longer NHS waiting times, and in schools, increased numbers of pupils with English as a second language doesn't seem to lower the performance for English speaking students – if anything, pupils in schools with lots of non-native speakers do slightly better.

4. What happens after Brexit?

Even before Brexit actually happens, immigration, especially from the EU, is already falling. As the economy slows, eurozone economies recover, and the UK appears a less welcoming and attractive place for immigrants, especially European ones. We still know very little about what a post-Brexit system will look like, except that it is likely to be considerably more restrictive for people coming from the EU.

However, there are some key points:

- Ending free movement is not primarily about border control. It does not seem likely that we would restrict EU nationals' right to enter the UK without a visa (any more than we do for Americans or Australians). So, controls will have to be applied by employers at the workplace (e.g. in the NHS, schools, by landlords and so on).

- It is often claimed that if the UK could impose restrictions on migration from the EU, the impact would be to reduce unskilled migration, while having no impact on skilled migration, or even allowing an increase. But immigration is not just a matter of the UK choosing migrants; migrants have to choose us. Even if we wish to remain open to skilled migrants from elsewhere in the EU post-Brexit, they may not choose to come here, or stay here. The sharp fall in the number of healthcare staff, especially nurses, coming from the EU is already evidence of this. In the short term, at least, Brexit is likely to reduce skilled migration.

JONATHAN PORTES

Jonathan Portes is Professor of Economics and Public Policy at King's College London. He served as Chief Economist at the Department for Work and Pensions from 2002-2008 and at the Cabinet Office from 2008-2011. From 2011-2015, he was Director of the National Institute of Economic and Social Research.

Section Two
UK Integration Stories

Muslims in Northern Ireland

Northern Ireland has one of the lowest Muslim populations in Europe. Around 4800 Muslims were recorded in the 2011 census. However, we estimate a more realistic figure is around 6000. There are no Muslim or BME majority areas in Northern Ireland. Due to the relatively small numbers of Muslims in Northern Ireland (around 0.4 per cent) many people have had little or no interaction with Muslims. According to the 2015 *NI Life* and *Times Survey* only around 9 per cent of the population have any daily or weekly contact with a Muslim.

Racially motivated crimes in Northern Ireland now exceed sectarian ones (PSNI, 2017), and a large proportion of these are against Muslims (Migrant Centre NI). Throughout 2017, Muslims in Northern Ireland have been a focus for Britain First rallies and videos. There have been acts of vandalism on Muslim (or perceived Muslim) businesses.

For the past three years, Community Eid celebrations have been the target for online abuse with local websites and Facebook pages hosting hundreds of xenophobic and anti-Muslim comments. The most prominent Facebook page 'Exposing Islam in Northern Ireland' was run by Belfast Councillor Jolene Bunting and her husband. It has since been closed down. Despite meeting members of the community on a visit to the Belfast Islamic Centre (BIC), Councillor Bunting continues to make controversial comments about Islam and Muslims.

In January 2018, BIC ran a survey, open to all Muslims in Northern Ireland, to get a better gauge of the issues facing Muslims in Northern Ireland. In our survey 53 per cent of respondents had received verbal abuse and 11 per cent physical abuse. Anecdotal accounts suggest most hate crimes against Muslims go unreported to authorities. During a talk on reporting hate crime at our ladies' coffee morning in January 2018, we discovered all 15 present had been victims of verbal or physical abuse. Only two incidents

Former Northern Ireland First Minister Peter Robinson pictured in June 2014 with members of Muslim community during his visit to the Belfast Islamic Centre in Wellington Park, South Belfast. Photo by Kelvin Boyes / Press Eye

had actually been reported to the police (both cases of criminal damage). Despite this, the majority of respondents to our survey felt comfortable expressing their religious identity in Northern Ireland (around 69 per cent), although around 22 per cent overall said this depended on the area they resided in.

It has to be highlighted that despite recent hate incidents, most Muslims in Northern Ireland feel that society is welcoming and tolerant. Northern Ireland is small, family orientated and relatively close knit. We have a very good relationship with the police. There is no Muslim or BME representation in Northern Ireland politics, in part due to its partisan nature, however Nationalist Parties and the Alliance Party have been particularly vocal in their support.

As a vital part of our work, BIC has an 'open door' policy and hosts weekly visits by organisations, schools, churches and individuals - challenging misconceptions and stereotypes.

Both BIC and NIMFA (Northern Ireland Muslim Family Association) take part in the Muslim Council of Britain's 'Visit My Mosque' initiative. After conversations at the 2017 'Visit My Mosque' day, BIC is now working to develop a 'Three Faiths Forum' which will take an active role in combating prejudice, Islamophobia and anti-Semitism.

Although people are concerned about the recent rise in hostility, the major issue for our community is the lack of a purpose-built mosque. Current centres are too small and as a result unable to provide the facilities and support our community desperately needs.

Isolation is a major problem in Northern Ireland, and many children are the only Muslims in their class or school. Around 8-10 men and women convert to Islam every year at BIC alone and many converts are active in the community. Unfortunately, some are estranged from their families as a result. Belfast hosts a sizeable number of Muslim refugees and asylum seekers who have complex needs. Mosques cannot be merely places of prayer, they need to be hubs offering spiritual, emotional, social and practical support.

Belfast Islamic Centre is the main contact point for Muslims in Northern Ireland. It has a weekend Islamic school for children, youth clubs, women's breakfast club and coffee morning, mums and tots, girl's self-defence classes, health seminars and various Islamic and Qur'an classes. It is currently setting up a small foodbank and distributes zakat money to around fifteen families and individuals a week. The centre is too small and no longer fit for purpose. BIC has bought a much larger building and is trying to raise £750,000 for its development.

NIMFA in Belfast run seminars and classes, often in conjunction with BIC. In towns around Northern Ireland, smaller mosques for daily prayers have been set up in houses or small warehouses: The HAWA Centre Dunmurry, Causeway Islam, Islamic Centre of Newtownards, Portadown Muslim Association, Newry Muslim Association and North West Islamic Society. Centres are open to all Muslims regardless of gender, ethnic group or sect.

Despite all our challenges, Muslims in Northern Ireland are largely a positive outward looking community. Survey respondents expressed a desire for us as Muslims to be more united and to be an example to society, in terms of manners and behaviour. To emulate the Prophet (peace and blessing be upon him) in our dealings with people. To engage, communicate and interact with the local community as much as we can and to work to break down stereotypes by action, charitable work and greater community involvement.

Recommendations

- Get the message out: We need to do more to highlight the positive impact Muslims have on society to counteract the common media narratives. We have attempted to be more proactive on social media and with local politicians to highlight the work that we do combined with our Visit My Mosque days.

- Have social programmes alongside religious activities: Not everyone has a supportive family network. Despite our limited space, our breakfast clubs and coffee mornings help reduce alienation and loneliness. We have a community iftar every day during Ramadan which really helps bring the community together.

- Get women involved: Many of our activities are organised and run by women. It has helped break down stereotypes when visiting groups realise women play key roles in our community.

- Get young people involved.

NAOMI GREEN

Naomi Green is from a conservative Evangelical Christian background and converted to Islam in 2006. She volunteers with the Belfast Islamic Centre and became a member of the Executive Committee before joining the staff in 2016. She is currently working to improve community relations and political representation for the Muslim community.

A Welsh Muslim Experience

In Wales there is a definite difference between the urban and suburban/rural areas. Cities such as Cardiff, Newport and Swansea have longstanding Muslim communities due to the historical coal ports of the region, and as such integration is far more advanced than in other areas. Racism exists, but ironically one is far more likely to hear anti-English sentiments than anti-immigrant, anti-black, or Islamophobic.

However, venture out of these centres only a few miles and the demographic changes drastically. Towns less than a twenty minute drive from the capital have a far less diverse population, and sadly it is in these locations that racism and other far-right ideologies are more likely to be taking hold. This can be seen in the recent European Referendum results, where ironically, the economically deprived areas that benefit the most from EU funding were the ones to vote to leave the EU, mainly due to the decidedly anti-immigration rhetoric pushed by some of the Leave campaigners.

In the wake of Darren Osborne's attack on the worshippers at Finsbury Park last Ramadan, many in Cardiff, Muslim and otherwise, were deeply shocked that 'one of our own' could do something so heinous. But amongst certain communities in the Valleys, on social media at least, posts implying that he didn't do a good enough job were frequently seen.

Specifics of the Welsh Environment That Have Helped or Hindered Integration

The South of Wales is diverse and cities are fairly small, which has helped the local communities to get to know one another. Perhaps the history of the Welsh people being subjugated by the English has given them a sense of justice, different from other parts of the UK.

However, the woeful state of the South-to-North transport links in Wales mean that Muslim communities living in the North are far more likely to form links with Manchester and Liverpool than with Cardiff. Also communities living in Mid and West Wales often cite feelings of isolation. There are growing communities in the southwest, such as Carmarthen and Pembrokeshire, but these have fairly easy access to the M4 corridor, something that those in the West and North lack.

Challenges faced by Muslim Communities

Speaking specifically of Cardiff and Newport, we have a disproportionate level of high school dropouts amongst Muslim youth. This often leads to economic deprivation, which in turn leads to illegal means of finding an income. The number of young Muslim men incarcerated for drug dealing for example is very high.

The fact that a few young men also ran away from home to travel to Syria to join the fighting there has been a black mark on the image and reputation of the community. Many feel the media unfairly drags out the story of those boys again and again, and as such we struggle to move on and present the true image of all the good work we are doing.

As is the case elsewhere in the UK, the feeling of living 'under a microscope' due to Prevent legislation and counter-extremism efforts, is keenly felt.

Examples of Good Practice

- The New Leaf project (now ended) worked to help ex-offenders re-integrate into the Muslim community, and to help heal rifts between former prisoners and their families. A huge rate of success was seen in reducing the rate of re-offending, but sadly the funding for this much needed project came to an end.

- The Muslim Council of Wales runs a youth leadership course, ILEAD, for young men and women aged 14-18 in Newport, and 16-18 in Cardiff. This aims to empower young people with the skills they need to grow into community leaders, to understand the importance of engaging with the wider community at the grassroots and policy making levels, and also to inspire them to strive in their educational aspirations.

- Dar ul-Isra Mosque holds various activities for the public, including participating in Visit My Mosque day, regular school visits, and Sharing Ramadan open iftar events.

- Many mosques hold halaqas (study circles) specifically aimed at the youth (ages 13+) for both boys and girls, which serve as a 'safe space' for young people to air their concerns and thoughts, without fear of judgement.

AMANDA MORRIS

Amanda Morris is the Administrative Executive and Media Liaison for the Muslim Council of Wales. She was previously National Head of Women's Engagement at MEND, and Chair of the Cardiff working group. Amanda has an MA in Islam in Contemporary Britain from Cardiff University, and also holds an MA in Japanese Applied Linguistics from SOAS.

A Brummie Muslim Experience

Birmingham is the second largest city in the UK, after London. Much like London, it is also an incredibly diverse and multi-cultural city. There are areas within the city where ethnic minority communities have clustered, and around 20 per cent of the city's population is of South Asian descent (mainly Indian, Kashmiri, Bangladeshi, Pakistani). There are also small Somali and Arab communities. Towards the inner city is the densest Muslim population which has also seen the biggest influx of refugee and asylum seeker populations.

With the bulk of the Muslim population centred towards inner Birmingham, and with the highest proportion of refugee populations also placed there, it is also the hub of Muslim involvement in charity projects. iCare is a department of the UK Islamic Mission (UKIM) focused on local community support projects, such as running food hubs. Sparkhill in South Birmingham, most recently known for being the location of the BBC television show 'Citizen Khan', is the location of two food hubs set up by UKIM iCare in collaboration with two local Churches. Within that setup, the volunteers communicate and integrate with those using the iCare Food Hub. This project has highlighted the sheer diversity of those needing to come to food hubs, with people coming from Romanian, Iranian, Yemeni, Pakistani, Indian, Nigerian and even European (French) backgrounds. It is also equally split between male and female users. Users of these iCare Food hubs include local people on low income requiring social and financial support until their next pay cheque.

These iCare Food Hubs highlight only part of the significant need within the wider Birmingham community to help those who have fallen through the cracks of social services and need immediate care. Despite receiving a limited amount of help from food banks and charities set up by both Muslim and other communities, there remains a significant demand for social welfare and support. In speaking to local female users, stories emerge of mothers having their children placed into care and feeling desperate and lonely.

Muslim Council of Britain

They highlight a desperate need for community which is another benefit of the food hub as it provides signposting to other services such as UKIM Ladies coffee mornings, within the Mosque, where women can speak confidentially about their situation and concerns.

Issues relating to crime centre predominantly around drugs and robberies along with more sophisticated organised crime; certainly, there is a gang culture which needs to be tackled, a situation exacerbated by continuing budgetary pressures on Police forces, who are already struggling. West Midlands Police are in the process of selling police buildings to raise funds. Criminality therefore remains an attraction for the young and unemployed, particularly as it offers access to cash quickly.

Challenges are most clearly observed, however, with young people struggling to get jobs following university graduation; this is hampered for many by their ethnicity, faith or gender.

Within the wider Birmingham community, there is an issue of lack of support for young people. Grants are no longer readily available for youth services and so there is a lack of spaces for children and young adults. Within Muslim communities, this problem is doubly felt; not only is there a lack of youth services, projects are often Lottery-funded. These are usually avoided by Muslim youth as they are seen as toxic and offer no credibility to the administering groups in question. This is why the role of mosques is so crucial; they are seen as safe places and trusted resources for many of these initiatives, without the stigma associated with Lottery.

Within Birmingham there remain many segregated communities. There have however been progressive moves to engage more effectively with wider communities. The community organising group 'Citizens UK' has done a fantastic job in bringing communities together to address common causes. This has been a successful and crucial step in breaking down barriers.

With regards to integration, this has proven to be challenging with the older generation of Muslim communities. However, the younger generation see fewer barriers, and have a much better and more effective understanding of discrimination and equality; this is in part due to the excellent job done by schools. Challenges are most clearly observed, however, with young people struggling to get jobs following university graduation; this is hampered for many by their ethnicity, faith or gender. There are some projects reaching out specifically to BAME communities with employment opportunities, such as HS2, which is a positive step. However, many Muslims continue to see labels applied to them from media discourse and rhetoric surrounding Muslims, and in turn experience the consequences of these labels.

As identified above, there is a large and diverse Muslim community in and around Birmingham. There are several external and internal challenges for the Muslim community, and work is being done to allow for ongoing progression. The Mayor of Birmingham Andy Street has however done well and had an overall positive impact.

Recommendations
- Employment: encourage investment into the area.

- Crime: more resources are needed to police and discourage youth through other initiatives.

- Co-ordinate communities more effectively e.g., organisations like Citizens UK.

- Mosques should continue to work together across ethnic and sectarian lines to work for the common cause e.g., Iftars during Ramadan for all.

- Political engagement: more needs to be done to get a voice which represents all demographics with people in power.

ADREES SHARIF

Adrees Sharif is Vice President of UK Islamic Mission's Midland Zone, and Head of Youth at Paigham-e-Islam Masjid in Sparkhill, Birmingham. He believes he has a duty to serve his community and wider society "for the greater good" and to help inculcate positive behaviours and relationships both within the Muslim community and wider society.

Integrating Blackburn's Muslims

Blackburn, one of Lancashire's larger towns with a population close to 120,000, has held a thriving Muslim population since the 1950s. The majority of the community is of South Asian ethnicity, largely Indian and Pakistani, with a growing Bangladeshi presence. As with other northern mill towns, and particularly those of East Lancashire, Blackburn has struggled in the socio-economic and employment sphere; however, in contrast to the rest, it has also fostered a thriving centre. We can look to the Muslim communities as having contributed to this upheaval against the harsh economic conditions of the north of England.

In terms of education, Tauheed School is a Muslim-run secondary school committed to educational excellence and British values. It is consistently ranked as one of the best schools in the country, with outstanding Ofsted reports for both Girls' and Boys' schools. Blackburn also has two dedicated Islamic colleges (Dar Al Ulooms), one each for boys and girls. These seek to produce British-born scholars, instilled with British values. The Muslim community has made contributions to the thriving business in Blackburn through a number of young entrepreneurs and family businesses, such as with Muslim entrepreneurs Zubair and Mohsin who co-founded Euro Garages. Branching further out, retail forecourts such as Star Tissue UK Limited have also emerged from the community.

Social activism and contribution remains strong amongst the Muslim community. The majority of mosques regularly contribute to food banks, and are also heavily involved in volunteering with or raising money for local hospices and East Lancashire hospitals. Examples of endeavours have included raising money to buy cardiac arrest machines and environmental clean-ups, in an effort to benefit wider society.

Challenges and limitations within the Muslim community have been identified by and discussed within the community themselves. Blackburn has been accused of being a particularly segregated town, with some areas being almost completely Muslim Asian. This gained particular prominence following the BBC Panorama documentary 'White Fright.' Several challenges and reasons behind the segregation exist; indeed certain communities are content to live in segregation, particularly in areas where local mosques offer facilities to Muslims in the area. The Panorama documentary also rightly touched on the phenomenon of 'white flight', whereby immigrants to industrial towns in the 1970s and 1980s settled in cheaper housing which white British residents left in protest or fear of change. This continues to happen, often with certain areas seen as 'too Asian' for white British residents, and often become less desirable neighbourhoods for property buyers. This is core to the difficulty in addressing residential segregation, and certainly requires more research as to the reasoning behind it. It is unclear whether this stems from rising Islamophobic sentiment, miseducation and poor portrayal of Muslims, or propaganda surrounding desirable characteristics of a residential area.

There is a nationwide housing crisis, and governmental cuts do not help encourage mixing within areas, although government work within schools to allow for more diverse populations is a positive move. Furthermore, it must be noted that one cannot easily socially engineer where people move, and clustering of populations from similar backgrounds is seen worldwide. Indeed, when Britons move abroad to Spain or other European countries, or to countries for employment purposes, they often cluster together in their own segregated communities within a country. One can go to whole neighbourhoods in United Arab Emirates and other cosmopolitan Middle Eastern countries and encounter only expatriate communities. It is therefore also a question as to whether segregation, despite the indisputable challenges, is the overwhelmingly negative result that it is often portrayed as being.

Further challenges have also been highlighted within the community. A Muslim female leadership presence is lacking, as is provision of equal space and equal voice for women both in community centres and pivotal decisions. Although the Lancashire Council of Mosques, which covers Blackburn, has recently established a women's forum, there remains a great deal to be done in terms of equity of space in mosques and promoting more female speakers and community leaders. A growing BME youth population also brings its own challenges, both in integration to society and equal access to employment and other opportunities. However as more Muslim populations move into what are considered middle-class areas, this is creating opportunities for social mobility and breadth of employment opportunity. Indeed, with all the challenges identified, there is a clear move in the right direction. Work has been focused on interfaith initiatives and community cohesion. Education is a strong point, both in Muslim schools providing excellent state education and institutions dedicated to Islamic teaching in a British context. Several young entrepreneurs from the Muslim community run businesses which serve wider communities. Recommendations for both Muslim communities and government intervention are outlined below, with a view to continuing to allow the community to flourish.

Recommendations

- Established Muslim organisations, both locally and from the South, have a duty to offer more support to young British Muslims.

- Active leadership with equity of opportunity amongst Muslims within the community, particularly gender equality and a spread of age.

- Governmental focus and integration on the resource-deplete North – representing the voice of British Muslims and investing in support for intercultural dialogue.

- Governmental intervention and aid in the housing crisis, through building housing to help curb 'white flight' and reduce overt segregation.

FAZ PATEL

Faz Patel is a social entrepreneur and an ex-Trade Union Chair for BME communities in Blackburn. He was awarded an MBE for work promoting community cohesion.

A View From the East End

There are many challenges in the East End that affect the lives of Muslim communities today. In the past we have seen a significant influx of Bangladeshi Muslim immigrants to the area who remained and settled in the East End developing their businesses, mosques and educational institutions. More recently we have seen Muslim immigrants from Somalia, Pakistan and parts of North Africa settling here making up a diverse and vibrant ethnic community.

In the past year we have witnessed far right extremist groups marching through the heart of the Muslim communities here in East London, exacerbating their fears and lack of belonging to this country. Episodes such as these serve as a painful reminder of racial tensions and attacks which were commonplace for the early Muslim immigrants. As the current generation venture out to seek educational and employment opportunities further afield, there are anxieties of racism and Islamophobia felt by their families and an apprehension in the choices they make due to this.

In the past, mosques and community centres have welcomed first and second generation immigrant women in a bid to provide safe supportive environments where they could access help, integrate into the wider community and become self sufficient. However recently we have seen a sharp increase in people seeking counselling, relating to anxiety and depression using our service, particularly amongst women. In an environment where issues such as gang violence, drugs and more recently acid attacks make up the reality of life here, simple things such as travelling cause huge anxiety in some.

Additionally, issues such as the cost of living and a housing shortage have had a detrimental effect on the Muslim community. The government's introduction of a benefit cap has forced some families out of Tower Hamlets and this in turn has had ramifications on the whole family support network. Whilst some have moved to neighbouring boroughs such as Redbridge, Barking and Newham, enabling connection and support amongst families within a reasonable travelling distance, others have moved further away where there are limited community links to their own and a lack of integration with the host community.

Issues such as the cost of living and a housing shortage have had a detrimental effect on the Muslim community.

Furthermore, many families who did move away from the East End to distance themselves from social problems such as drug and knife crime, found that these issues were still prevalent elsewhere and without the community support they had, found themselves feeling further isolated. People gain strength and hope from a sense of community and belonging. Integration is a two way process and those that have forged meaningful interactions with others are found to be happier and more confident.

Organisations such as TELCO (The East London Communities Organisation, a chapter of Citizens UK), the Jagonari Centre and many others have been instrumental in providing integrated services and programmes. TELCO brings together diverse communities committed to working together for social justice and a common good. Their campaigns for a Living wage, Housing and City Safe Zones demonstrate the powerful work they do.

Similarly, the Tower Hamlets Interfaith Forum has facilitated partnerships between faith groups and secular organisations allowing a platform for these groups to coexist and work together for the benefit of our community. The Tower Hamlets 'No Place For Hate' Forum is another initiative which supports and protects the community whilst deterring hate crime and challenging those who perpetrate it.

Religious places of worship have increasingly become places where community issues are expressed. Mosques being accessible have helped dispel myths of radical activities going on behind closed doors. The Muslim Council of Britain's annual 'Visit my Mosque' initiative is one that encourages and supports over 200 mosques to open their doors to the public as way of integration with the wider community. However, here at the East London Mosque we open

Sufia Alam, Manager of the Maryam Centre at the East London Mosque speaks to HRH The Princess Royal visiting the institution in 2017. Photo: East London Mosque

our doors daily to schools, colleges, universities and host visitors nationwide and abroad to engage and learn about our religion. It is through these increasingly important initiatives that communities come together with mutual respect. Integration has to be a two way process; social mixing has to be initiated and continued.

The media plays a key role in the misrepresentation of Muslims with their negative portrayal on a daily basis, instilling fear in those who have limited contact with them. It is imperative that there are more balanced and positive news stories demonstrating an accurate picture of Muslim participation in British society.

As Muslims we need to assert our abilities, skills, successes and achievements to create the leaders of tomorrow that take our whole community together with them. We are too divided amongst ourselves and tend to be overly critical of others who have differing views.

We must go back to the example of the Prophet (peace and blessings be upon him); dispel the prejudices we have within our own faith communities to coexist in a community that is tolerant of our schools of thought, cultures and fundamental beliefs. We must know our religion in the way it was sent to us and teach it to the next generation with tolerance and understanding that is appropriate in the era we live in.

Muslim Council of Britain

We need to acknowledge our children's journey is incredibly different to the one our parents faced. The older generation had resilience and survival instincts at a time when there were no integration programmes, translators and community leaders that represented them. They did not feel part of a British society. However our children do and they have choices. We must listen to our children and nurture them. We must not teach them to fear or reflect our own fears upon them. We must be educated about our rights and have a much broader dialogue.

Examples of good practice

- Visit My Mosque.

- Visiting the sick: chaplaincy work in hospitals.

- Mother and daughter events.

- Seminars on the rights of women, children, wives, husbands, neighbours in the Qur'anic context.

- Regular tea and tours.

- Feeding the homeless, food bank initiatives organised by Muslims.

- Iftar gatherings.

- Lunch clubs and coffee mornings.

SUFIA ALAM

Sufia Alam is the Centre Manager at the Maryam Centre, part of the East London Mosque Trust. She has worked in the third sector for the past 20 years. Sufia has worked to actively empower women in the community and has a background in community leadership

An Identity Crisis in Bradford?

The following is a report of a consultation session the Muslim Council of Britain held with a cross section of British Muslims in Bradford.

The threats to a thriving and engaged Muslim community are many. In a consultation and in conversations with Muslims across the city, one of the most commonly cited problems was institutional racism. Nowhere sees this more acutely than densely populated inner city areas. Whilst representation in the political scene in Bradford has been relatively successful, when it comes to senior management of Bradford's institutions, the picture is still woefully different with barely any progression for Muslims who have worked there for decades.

There is a deeper problem with the terminology of 'integration' itself, and the capacity it has to 'other' large swathes of the population. One young person articulates this sentiment in the following words: 'I'm already British, I recognise myself as British but if the government and other agencies are saying integrate – it's telling me I need to lose some aspect of my identity and assume additional aspects recognised by the government.'

Half of all British Muslims are under the age of 25, with a third under the age of 15. By 2020 Bradford will be the youngest city in Europe; 50 per cent of the population will be under the age of 25. When these young people are told that despite being born and raised in the UK, British values are something they're yet to adopt, it's no surprise this leads to the fuelling of an already polarised identity crisis.

As Naz Shah MP has consistently said: 'There is zero conflict between my Muslim values and "British" values, as frankly speaking, my Muslim values are shared values regardless of faith; based on human values of love, care and mutual respect and support for mankind. This is unlike "British values" which change over time depending on the decade. These haven't always been about equality, at one point were anti-people of colour, anti-gay and anti-women. Someone needs to define what British actually means.'

The current language of integration imposes a responsibility on one segment of the population to integrate into British society, but there is no such thing as a one-way street to community cohesion.

'We are here, because you were there.'

There is a reluctance to acknowledge and critique the British Empire, its colonial actions, motivations and role in the presence of many immigrants and their descendants here today. This translates into unease around present-day foreign policy, as one participant put it, there needs to be 'absolute identification of the way foreign policy treats people across the globe. There are days when I think as a person – why would I want to integrate with a country that does that to people?'

There is little to no real acknowledgement of immigrant contributions as the UK scrambles to make sense of borders and controls post-Brexit, deciding value by their economic contributions. Has there ever been a commitment to endorsing the contributions of immigrants as essentially 'British', barring Mo Farah's gold medals?

It cannot be overstated how much of an effect Islamophobia and anti-Muslim discrimination has had on Muslims being able to access different sectors, professions and services. From disparities in education, employment, media, public life to social media bullying and outbursts of street attacks; there has never been an adequate response from the government in providing a national legislative framework to uphold its own equality laws and obligations, with regards to protecting Muslims from discrimination.

There is a risk of misunderstanding Islamophobia as a passing trend brought on by events such as terrorist attacks. While there is a backlash in the aftermath, it's important to note that institutionalised Islamophobia is much broader and deeply rooted than these outbursts. As one Bradford resident noted, 'every definition of Islamophobia explains it as a pathological or psychological phenomenon, but no – it is a social, political and economic phenomenon.'

It is argued that through the lens of counter-extremism and counter-terrorism, the government has led the way in rendering Muslims a suspect community. This has paved the way for the categorisation of Muslims as 'moderate' and 'extreme', for Muslim charities to be investigated under suspicions of funding terrorism and for public figures to be considered not fit for their duties because of their religion.

It's highly telling that the Chair of the Independent Press Standards Organisation, when being questioned by a Parliamentary committee, refused to acknowledge sensationalised phrases like 'The Muslim Problem' as the language of hatred. Naz Shah MP states there is 'absolutely no question about Islamophobia passing the dinner table test. It passed the Parliament test a while ago.'

> *By 2020 Bradford will be the youngest city in Europe...When these young people are told that despite being born and raised in the UK, British values are something they're yet to adopt, it's no surprise this leads to the fuelling of an already polarised identity crisis.*

A facet often missing from all discussions of integration is class. The alleviation of poverty by way of targeted investment in education, employment and housing to name but a few areas in particular would be an excellent starting point to try to redress a societal imbalance of power and wealth creation.

Despite this, there are pressing issues within Muslim communities that need addressing. External barriers keep Muslims on the defensive, unable to be proactive in recognising and tackling concerns. Challenges around Islamic education and the role of mosques in communities, mental health and misogyny are rarely afforded the importance they deserve for internal discussions. A delicate balance must be struck by our representatives, both institutional and individual leaders. They must be fit for purpose in serving communities and enabling these discussions to happen appropriately.

Many fear speaking out due to a weaponisation of societal

problems. 'We're always having to be defensive. We can't be proactive – the whole thing is loaded and we're constantly fighting a battle.' Misogyny is a real problem across society, but it's highlighted extraordinarily more frequently as a Muslim problem in an attempt to pathologise Muslim men as motivated by hatred and extremism. Not only does this leave Muslim women abandoned, but it also abuses their political agency to prove points by the far right and Islamophobes within and outside government.

It goes without saying that there needs to be a shift away from the language of integration, towards equality, diversity and respect. These should be the key tenets of any debate about enabling and empowering Muslims to play a full role in British society. Widespread discrimination and anti-Muslim sentiments are preventing Muslims from making this contribution to the prosperity and wellbeing of British society. The way forward on many of the above areas needs to be developed with full participation and involvement of Muslim communities up and down the country. Any cultural change must be widespread, involving all corners of British society, it must evolve organically and most importantly, it must be grassroots community-led, not imposed.

SAMAYYA AFZAL

Samayya Afzal is an activist based in Bradford, with experience in the higher education sector. She has held a series of elected student union positions, including the National Executive Council of the National Union of Students. She has also worked in diversity development, curating exhibitions related to the South Asian diaspora. Samayya currently works at the Muslim Council of Britain as Community Engagement Manager.

A Scottish Muslim Story

As with the UK as a whole, the origins of Scotland's established Muslim communities lie in the large-scale settlement of mainly South Asian Muslims in the aftermath of World War II. Many of the challenges and anxieties associated with the Muslim integration experience in Scotland can be said to mirror those in other parts of the UK. Two issues at the centre of the current integration debate are racism and Islamophobia, and the integration of recent refugee arrivals. Both of these issues intersect in various ways, with the settlement of refugees being used to stoke racism and Islamophobia, and Islamophobia (particularly in moments of political tension) being used to demonise refugees.

Islamophobia in particular, ranges from the everyday experience of 'street-level' abuse or discrimination, reported experiences of Islamophobic bullying within schools and educational spaces,[1] in the workplace,[2] through to far-right activity in the form of provocative demonstrations and criminal attacks on individuals and buildings. The integration of refugees remains at the top of the agenda – with around 40% of refugees from Syria arriving in the UK being re-settled in Scotland, it continues to be an area of contention, but also one of pride for many Scots.

Scotland's small Muslim population can perhaps be counted as one factor which has facilitated integration. Numbering at just under 80,000, and constituting around 1.5 per cent of the total Scottish population,[3] the overwhelming proportion of Scotland's Muslims reside in and around the urban areas of Glasgow, Edinburgh, Dundee and Aberdeen. However, the population is relatively sparsely distributed within these urban regions, with only minimal 'clustering' in parts of Glasgow – thus concerns around segregated communities, such as those typically associated with towns in the north of England, have not arisen.

Other factors that have arguably supported the impression of easy integration include the economic self-sufficiency of many among

Scotland's Muslims – with high levels of self-employment and an increasingly highly educated, youthful population – the idea of a Muslim community being an economic asset rather than a liability, with much to offer in terms of talent, expertise and affluence has aided integration. It has been argued that a history of sectarian tensions between Catholics and Protestants in Scotland has 'cushioned' Muslims and other minorities from hostility. At the same time, South Asian Muslims and other 'new Scots' are able to share in sentiments of 'Anglophobia' which has helped minorities to find 'common cause' with the wider Scottish population – to more readily take on a Scottish identity.[4]

> *Politically engaged Scottish Muslims regularly cite a genuine sense of identification with an open Scottish national identity, in which they hold an equal stake.*

Though still enduringly widespread in popular discourse, the proverbial 'no problem here' narrative is increasingly being questioned by academic research. Surveys have regularly indicated unease among 'White' Scots towards a growing Muslim presence,[5] suggesting that levels of integration within and between communities still have some way to go. And while economic and educational achievements are to be celebrated, the proportion of ethnic minorities in senior-level professional employment and the civil service are abysmally low.

There are specific challenges to integration that are faced by Muslim communities. One of these is the notably high rate of economic inactivity among Muslim women. This can partly be attributed to a higher birth rate – thus, a greater proportion of young dependents in the household. However, it is clear that more can be done to boost employability among Muslim women. This includes initiatives to facilitate this, by equipping and supporting Muslim women to deal with obstacles in society and address any barriers within their communities as well.

The Scottish Government's active promotion of an inclusive 'civic nationalism' has had broad appeal to a diverse range of ethnic and religious minorities. Politically engaged Scottish Muslims regularly cite a genuine sense of identification with an open Scottish national identity, in which they hold an equal stake. There are salutary lessons in this experience for politicians and government agencies across the UK who seek to address problems of social segregation. Furthermore, initial studies of the 'New Scots' refugee integration strategy suggest that its promotion of inter-sectoral and inter-agency collaboration has been a noteworthy success.[6]

Notwithstanding this positive rhetoric, the recently launched Cross Party Group on Racism and Islamophobia within the Scottish Parliament has shone a light on the persistence of stark prejudices and inequalities in many areas of Scottish public life, while ongoing research at the University of Edinburgh indicates a continuing 'trend of discrimination' faced by BME Scots.[7] Without strong action to acknowledge and combat worrying levels of racism and Islamophobia by local and national Scottish governmental agencies, the translation of 'civic nationalism' to the everyday experience of integration is at real risk.

KHADIJAH ELSHAYYAL

Dr Khadijah ElShayyal is a Post-Doctoral Research Fellow at the University of Edinburgh. She finished her PhD at Royal Holloway, University of London, in 2013.

Notes

1. Dean, Samena, 'Islamophobia in Edinburgh Schools' (Scotland Against Criminalising communities, 2017), Finlay, Robin et al 'Muslim youth and political participation in Scotland' (Newcastle University, 2017).

2. For example, see accounts in Syswerda, Rebecca, 'The Role of the 'Other' Woman in Shaping the Subjectivities of Recent Muslim Migrant Women to Scotland' in Hopkins, Peter (ed.), Scotland's Muslims (EUP, 2017).

3. Elshayyal, Khadijah, 'Scottish Muslims in Numbers: understanding Scotland's Muslims through the 2011 Census' (University of Edinburgh, 2016).

4. Bonino, Stefano, Muslims in Scotland: the making of community in a post-9/11 world (EUP, 2017).

5. Hussain, Asifa and William Miller, Multicultural Nationalism: Islamophobia, Anglophobia and devolution (OUP, 2006); Homes, Amy et al 'Muslim integration in Scotland' (Ipsos Mori Scotland and the British Council, 2010).

6. Ostergaard, Liv, 'New Scots: Integrating Refugees into Scottish Communities', European Journal of Public Health, 27:3 (November 2017).

7. 'Prejudice against black and ethnic Scots 'widespread'' <https://www.ed.ac.uk/news/2017/prejudice-against-black-and-ethnic-scots-widesprea> (Accessed 22 Feb 2018)

Welcoming Refugees

Integration is a core part of the public debate around immigration, ethnic and faith diversity in the UK. Through integration, refugees become active members of British society. This matters – to refugees themselves, to the communities in which they are resettled, and to wider society.

Refugees are a diverse group in relation to their country of origin, education and employment along with the length of time and experiences they have had in the UK. Failures of integration can take multiple forms; including social segregation, community tensions between migrants and host communities, educational under-achievement and high levels of unemployment. Perceptions that migrants have not integrated can also exacerbate negative public attitudes.

Integration is a two-way street, which, if it is to be achieved, requires both migrants and host communities to find ways of engaging. A lack of integration is often most apparent in areas of high deprivation, which points to the need to address structural barriers, including a lack of economic opportunities. A compounded element of discrimination, owing to religion and ethnicity, is a key consideration, with refugees often seen as the 'other' or perceived as a threat. Tailored support for refugees facing hate, recognising cultural variations and accommodating potential language barriers would be a welcome initiative.

Social Contact

Social contact is a key consideration for successful integration. Organic interaction fosters a sense of togetherness, breaking down misconceptions and social divides between 'them' and 'us'. It enriches the lives of all and develops collective agency within communities. Mutual trust helps foster democratic participation, economic advancement and a thriving civil society, whereas its absence can lead to civic hostilities, communal division and segregation. Deeper community relations are thus vital in developing a more united, cohesive and stronger nation.

Meaningful social contact fosters a sense of belonging for refugees, helps them learn English and learn about life in the UK, along with combating isolation and loneliness that some refugees experience. Initiatives such as Refugee Week and Cultural Awareness Events are effective in celebrating diversity, bringing together refugees and local communities, as well as developing greater cultural competence. These could be held more regularly to increase education and develop mutual respect.

Across the UK, civil society and faith organisations ensure that those who arrive through the Vulnerable Person's Resettlement Scheme (VPRS) and Community Sponsorship Scheme have been welcomed into the community and introduced to activities that may help build friendships.

The Community Sponsorship scheme in particular, forges social links between a refugee family and the sponsoring organisation (often a faith group with large membership), and brings many people in contact with refugees.

But those who have not come through these schemes have comparatively little social contact.

A key challenge is how we enable social contact between refugees and wider society, and this is an area where Muslim organisations could take a lead. From sports, to cookery, gardening and arts & crafts, the provision of communal activities could enhance social contact.

Education and Employment
For many refugees, a lack of fluency in the English language, along with not possessing UK recognised qualifications are key factors hindering their ability to find work. Across the UK, there are reported shortages of ESOL provision, and there is a danger that delays in starting English language classes will have a negative impact on wellbeing and integration.

Refugees learn English through informal classes, as well as everyday social interactions with English speakers. Again, mosques and community groups could take a leading role here by providing spaces and opportunities where social contact and conversations could take place.

Refugee dispersal has generally been to areas where housing is cheaper and more readily available. Unsurprisingly this is often in poorer parts of the UK where work is harder to find. For young refugees who arrive in the UK having had their education interrupted, there is a lack of schemes that enable them to access suitable education; and therefore, they may be at higher risk of unemployment and social exclusion.

When it comes to finding employment, many are reliant on social networks. Many refugees will have left behind successful and highly skilled careers, and will struggle adjusting to the fact that their qualifications and at times experience will not be sufficient to secure a similar job. Communities could provide support through mentorship, apprenticeships and internships along with traditional CV and interview support.

Additional Challenges

For many refugees attempting to rebuild their lives in the UK, one of the main barriers to full integration is the constant worry and/or guilt over family members left behind. A strength of the long-running Canadian private sponsorship scheme is that it allows for 'naming', whereby sponsoring groups can specify the family unit they want to resettle. We are hopeful that as the UK's sponsorship scheme develops, this area will be carefully considered.

Examples of Good Practice

Across the UK, there are countless examples of Muslim groups, communities and civil society working to make a difference and supporting refugees and migrants. The Muslim diaspora are also well placed to understand the challenges of migration, and the specific cultural challenges some refugees may experience.

In response to the Syrian refugee crisis, people from across the country have organised to create welcoming communities, forming over 90 Refugees Welcome campaign groups. Muslim individuals and groups have been actively involved in the Refugees Welcome movement through membership of Citizens UK, pushing the government to increase the number of refugees they pledged to resettle resulting in the commitment of 20,000 by 2020.

Volunteers have been central to the effort to welcome unaccompanied minors, families resettled under VPRS and through community sponsorship; providing language skills, acting as landlords, furnishing accommodation, hosting community events and more.

There are numerous examples of where Muslims have made a significant difference to the successful integration of refugees, recognising that interventions are needed from the onset to build resilience and confidence.

Organisations such as the Amina Muslim Women's Resource Centre in Dundee have developed its Refugee support project, matching resettled families with a Refugee Support Officer working with them. They support individuals in gaining confidence and independence, speaking English, entering employment and have many volunteers who have strong cultural awareness as well as local knowledge, and contribute to the welcoming atmosphere in the city.

The Sufra Food Bank in North West London has taken responsibility to provide food and supplies for refugees brought into the borough by Brent Council. They are also actively looking for work placements for newly arrived Syrian refugees who are skilled in plumbing, painting, mechanics and construction.

Islamic centres such as the KSIMC of Birmingham, the East London Mosque and many more are working towards becoming a community sponsor to transform the lives of a refugee family. More mosques and charities should consider this to welcome and resettle vulnerable refugees. Organisations such as Sponsor Refugees have been established to support such groups.

ESMAT JERAJ

Esmat Jeraj is a community activist. Professionally, she is a community organiser with Citizens UK, working for the Sponsor Refugees Foundation promoting community sponsorship of refugees affected by the Syrian conflict. She led a national commission exploring barriers to Muslim participation in public life, and authored its report *The Missing Muslims: Unlocking British Muslim Potential for the Benefit of All*, which explored issues around integration, employment disadvantage, anti-Muslim prejudice and the role of Muslim institutions.

Section Three
Enabling Muslims to Play Their Full Part

Remove Barriers to Social Mobility

At its most basic level, the idea of social mobility is simple. It is the notion that in the society in which you grow up, you're given the best possible start in life.

The best possible start to allow you to develop your abilities as best you can as a human being. To test your abilities in the right environment and setting, to aspire to go as far as your talents will allow you, free from discrimination and prejudice standing in your way.

Just 7% of the UK population attend independent schools. And yet their alumni make up 71% of senior judges, 43% of newspaper columnists and 33% of MPs. The least disadvantaged students are six times more likely to enter a highly selective university than the most disadvantaged, according to the Social Mobility Foundation Annual Review 2015-2016.

Today, Britain is in the grip of a social mobility crisis. So much of your future success, or not, is pre-determined by your social status, the parents to whom you're born and the schools you attend.

Children from high income backgrounds who show signs of low academic ability by the age of 5 are 35% more likely to be high earners as adults than children from poorer families who show early signs of high ability.

Young people today are fast becoming a lost generation, facing even more difficult challenges than previous generations, and the first since the Second World War to face poorer prospects than their parents did. To say nothing of the multiple of deficits faced by people belonging to minority groups, women and those who have a combination of the aforementioned statuses.

The Challenges
Class politics and skewed privilege have also distorted the picture of what we are attempting to do, blighting the possibilities to transform society and the lives of many of its citizens

One of the key ways to ensure that we improve social mobility is to find more tangible ways to give people a stake in society. Young people especially, have to believe that they have a future and stake in a society which is beneficial to them and those around them.

If a young person does not feel that the society in which they're growing up has a place for them, they're unlikely to want to invest in it, they are less likely to be properly integrated and they're less likely to grow up to be productive and giving members of society.

> *One of the key ways to ensure that we improve social mobility is to find more tangible ways to give people a stake in society.*

There are multiple barriers to becoming socially mobile. They include:

- Lack of access to a quality, fulfilling and challenging education;

- An environment at home in which you're unable to eat well, sleep soundly and have the space to do your work, reflect and be positive;

- A community where there is a poverty of ambition, where you're encouraged to lower your sights and the simple pursuit of dreaming of a better future is either not possible or positively discouraged;

- Discrimination and prejudice if you're a minority can often exacerbate many of the aforementioned reasons, making any possibility even starker.

This list is not meant to be exhaustive.

Muslim communities in particular at the moment face a particularly unique challenge. British Muslims are more likely to be growing up in the most deprived wards in the country, where resources and provisions are either inadequate or non-existent.

These communities may well have strong family bonds but these links can only get them so far. A visible minority under constant and hostile scrutiny in sections of the media and in the minds of non-

Muslims has similarly created a climate of suspicion and mutual distrust.

These are some recommendations on the way forward;

- More understanding and acceptance that education is not the panacea or the sole answer to improving social mobility; much more is required;

- More efforts are required to actively encourage the mixing of minority and majority communities; this will help break down barriers, build more understanding and neutralise so much prejudice;

- A more open and visible availability of information for parents and guardians who may wish to help their children, but do not have access to the resources or knowhow;

- Mentoring schemes which are supposed to last for a significant period of time, in order to ensure that many children from deprived backgrounds have sustained support and guidance for years to come;

- A society striving for a setting/climate pursuant to genuine equality of opportunity.

HASHI MOHAMED

Hashi Mohamed came to Britain as a nine-year-old unaccompanied refugee from Kenya, following the collapse of the Somali state in 1991. One of 12 children, speaking little English, he attended some of London's 'worst performing schools', and was raised exclusively on state benefits. Today, Hashi is one of the UK's leading junior barristers and a member of The Honourable Society of Lincoln's Inn. Hashi also presents documentaries on BBC Radio 4.

Challenge Loneliness

Loneliness is a subjective experience of perceived social isolation which is likely at some stage to come to us all, alone or otherwise, young or old. Statistics collated last year by The Jo Cox Commission on Loneliness paint a stark picture of loneliness in the UK. Over 9 million adults say they are always or often lonely. On any given day, half of all disabled people feel lonely. More than 3.5 million people aged over 65 say that the television is their main source of company.

While loneliness as a phenomenon is nothing new, there is reason to believe it is becoming more widespread in modern Britain. Today, we are more likely to live alone than previous generations. Remote working means some of us rarely see our colleagues face-to-face. Profound socioeconomic inequalities can mean that despite walking the same streets, we sometimes live in different worlds.

Commonly triggered by life's moments of transition, loneliness can seriously harm our health. Physically, loneliness is worse for us than obesity and as bad for us as smoking 15 cigarettes a day. Mentally, it is a recipe for anxiety and stress and can lead to depression and dementia. Three quarters of GPs say that they see a handful of patients every day whose main problem is that they are lonely. Those who are lonely visit their doctors more frequently, spend longer in hospital and find it harder to recover and heal.

Loneliness can stifle and drain us as individuals, making us less productive and damaging the country's economy, but it also affects us in our communities, causing us to withdraw and disengage from one another. At a communal level, loneliness erodes empathy, undermining efforts at cohesion. Loneliness limits our ability to relate to one another and find shared ground. Instead of seeing we have more in common than that which divides us, we recede into our own corners, coming to view other identities with distrust. We put up walls when we should be building bridges. Paradoxically then, when people need to make new friends the most, they are often least able to do so, especially across perceived divides. In the capital, by way of illustration, over half of London's immigrants say loneliness is their biggest challenge when it comes to integration.

Over half of London's immigrants say loneliness is their biggest challenge when it comes to integration.

Britain's Muslim Communities are not Immune

Many Muslims in modern Britain are lonely too. Muslim teenagers are no less likely to be bullied on social media than their non-Muslim classmates, a new Muslim mother can feel as isolated at home alone with her baby as any other mum, and a lonely Muslim granddad can be too proud to admit it, just like any other. In some respects, Britain's Muslims are well equipped to avert loneliness. For instance, we feel part of a billion-strong global ummah, come together for prayer and tend not to live in care homes.

On the other hand, British Muslims may not go to the pub after lectures or work, are less likely to have dogs to walk as pets and may not feel comfortable talking openly about their feelings. Some first generation Muslim migrants to the UK may not speak great English, which is bound to leave them isolated. In certain Muslim communities, mixing with people of the opposite gender is limited as well. Often these barriers are in fact more cultural than religious. Regardless, where socialising is stigmatised, loneliness can follow.

But Loneliness can be overcome

Our best defence against loneliness is a meaningful connection with other human beings. We all need to connect with fellow travellers on our journey through life, just as the Prophet Mohammed – peace be upon him – had his own companions, the sahaba. Reciprocal relationships sustain our bodies, hearts and minds, making us feel valued and worthwhile. Even fleeting encounters with one another can ward off feelings of loneliness. When it comes to conversations, 'five a day' would go a long way and provides a memorable mantra. There are circumstances where we do talk to strangers, for instance when it snows. We need to recreate that dynamic, whatever the weather. Seen this way, starting a conversation with a neighbour or a fellow passenger can be an act of community service.

Giving, more than taking, lends us purpose. That is one reason why volunteering can be such a force for good. Voluntary and community groups then have a valuable role to play, empowering people to support others. They may also be well placed to help older people harness nostalgia to positive ends: telling one's own stories can be validating. From men's sheds to lunch clubs and reminiscence cafes, from neighbourly door-knocks to community allotments and intergenerational film-nights, charities up and down the country are already doing some tremendous work which can be built upon.

Companies too can make a difference: employers can support their workers to interact with one another, creating an environment conducive to kindness. A more personal approach may be good for business too. There are many private and third sector organisations that could play a role in helping us to connect.

The public sector has an important contribution to make too, without pretending there is some magic lever in Whitehall we can pull. Local authorities' planners can help to design loneliness out of our built environment and public realm. NHS doctors can do more social prescribing. Members of Parliament can argue for public policy to tackle loneliness, such as more relational content in national curricula or more funding for English language classes for refugees.

Some Steps to Take

The Government has begun to respond to the challenge by appointing a new minister to draw up a cross-departmental strategy for addressing loneliness in our society, devising a new set of national metrics to assess its effectiveness and releasing some funding to support initiatives in the community tackling isolation on the ground. Here are some specific suggestions for actions which Muslims in Britain could take to help take on loneliness in our communities and in society at large:

- Host communal iftars during Ramadan for local people of every faith and none.

- Throw open mosques' doors as part of the annual 'Visit My Mosque' initiative.

Muslim Council of Britain

- Ensure mosques and communities are genuinely accessible to disabled people.

- Run drop-in services at mosques for homeless people.

- Train native British imams who are fluent in English.

- Offer English for Speakers of Other Languages courses.

- Support divorcees – especially divorced women – in the community.

- Set up schemes to ensure that elderly neighbours are visited by members of the community during periods of cold weather, and beyond.

- Assist young people to be safe, confident and resilient online.

- Seek the support of local and national government for initiatives that look to foster everyday connections.

Taking such steps would make a real difference, demonstrating what engines of social capital faith institutions can be. Beating loneliness is not beyond us, but there is no shortcut: it will happen one conversation at a time. If we British Muslims do nothing else, let us simply remember that in Islam it is an act of charity – sadaqah – to smile.

ANDY HULL

Since 2010, Andy has been an elected councillor for Highbury West in the London Borough of Islington. The ward he represents is home to Arsenal FC, London Metropolitan University, The Holloway Masjid and Finsbury Park Mosque. Last year, he worked as a consultant on The Jo Cox Commission on Loneliness.

Making Education the Key to Integration

Education, it has been said, has four pillars – learning to be, learning to know, learning to do and learning to live with others. In these four ways, education is a force for healthy, mature and positive integration. To educate a child, it has also been said, requires a whole village – teachers in schools and colleges, but also lots of other people as well.

For the vast majority of human beings the first person in the village to take you in hand, and to educate you and integrate you, is your mother. Then of course there are others in the village too – your father and family, and various neighbours. In due course there is a primary school and secondary school, and further or higher education, and continuing education throughout your life. All these are agents of integration. You are grateful, but also sometimes wary and worried, and resistant. Hopefully but not necessarily, integration is healthy, mature and positive.

For parents, there are so many questions. Do we send our children to religious schools or to secular schools? Either way, how do we balance our various and sometimes conflicting duties and desires in relation to our children? For example, we want our children to be successful but not arrogant, happy but not complacent, slow to anger but not merely submissive, independent but not insensitive or uncaring. How do we warn our children about real dangers but not frighten them with fantasies? Protect and guide them, but not smother or imprison them? How do we help them navigate their way through the influences, inspirations and pressures they encounter daily? So many questions, no easy answers.

Muslim young people in Britain may have to find their way amidst the following influences, amongst others:

• Family life, and within these expectations, how young people should behave towards their elders, and expectations about gender roles.

Muslim Council of Britain

- The expectations and requirements of the mainstream education system.

- The mosque and mosque-based education, as compared with mainstream schools.

- New trends in Islamic theology and spirituality, particularly as developed in Europe and the United States.

- Street culture and youth culture, including drugs and other risk-taking behaviour, and lack of deference towards tradition and authority.

- Currents and strands of thought loosely known as 'extremism', 'political Islam', 'fundamentalism', 'Islamism' or 'radicalisation'.

Ofsted... appears to be less and less aware of this climate [of hostility towards Muslims]

Working on these issues, it is crucial to recognise, this takes place within a climate of suspicion and hostility towards Muslims in wider society. The climate has existed for a long time but appears to have become even more serious since the referendum in Britain on Brexit in 2016, and since the election of Donald Trump as the President of the United States.

In the education system in England there are many signs that Ofsted, the body responsible for inspecting and improving schools, appears to be less and less aware of this climate, and conversely has a greater inclination to make it worse.

If integration of Muslims into the education system and wider society is to be improved and strengthened, the following points and arguments need to be addressed.

1. There have recently been major improvements nationally in the educational achievement of pupils from Islamic backgrounds, and nationally there is no longer a gap between the achievement of Muslim pupils and the average for all pupils. But these improvements and greater equality of outcome are not evenly distributed throughout the country, and there continues to be

a need, particularly outside London and the south east, for attainment gaps to be narrowed and closed.

2. There needs to be more recognition in schools of British Muslim identities, more attention to issues of bilingualism, more commitment to the human right to freedom of religion, greater religious literacy amongst teachers and educational managers, more attention to Islamophobia, and closer relationships with parents and local communities.

3. There is a need for more Muslims to be involved actively in school governance and leadership, in educational policy-making and decision-making, and in the general educational workforce at all levels, particularly senior levels.

4. Ofsted and the Department for Education should take much more seriously than they in fact do, their public sector equality duty, to have due regard for the need to eliminate discrimination, advance equality of opportunity and foster good relations.

5. There is an urgent need to challenge, combat and resist Islamophobia. If politicians and educational leaders do not strenuously challenge Islamophobia in all its forms, young Muslims may feel that attempts they make to be active citizens are neither invited nor welcome. Equally unfortunately, their confidence and self-esteem may be damaged. They need to appreciate that Islam is not the cause of Islamophobia and they need moral, intellectual and emotional strength to resist and oppose it. This involves taking pride in their heritage and refusing to see themselves as helpless victims.

Few people are in a position to address all of these needs with equal urgency. All, however, are part of the village where the young learn how to be, to know, to do and to live with others. All have a part to play.

ROBIN RICHARDSON

Robin Richardson worked as a teacher and consultant for the Department of Education on equalities. He contributed to the seminal publication "Islamophobia: a challenge for us all" in 1997 and now runs the Insted consultancy, specialising in equality and diversity.

Housing and Integration

We know that Muslims are more likely to live in more deprived housing conditions than non-Muslims: based on 2011 census data, 35% of Muslim households are overcrowded, lack at least one bedroom, do not have central heating or have to share a kitchen or bathroom. In the total population the figure is 13%: a lot of housing deprivation for a rich country like Britain, but significantly lower. And no other faith group has similar levels of deprivation.

But the same figures can reveal a more complex story. Housing deprivation is usually associated with particular ethnic minority groups, with all more likely to be housing deprived than the white British groups.

Those with the highest proportion experiencing housing disadvantage are black African (43%) and Bangladeshi (42%). Muslims within these ethnic groups also have higher levels of housing disadvantage (48% and 55%), along with those described as 'black other' (58%). And within these, some communities in some areas face even worse conditions. A 2009 report on Somalis in north and east London found:

> 'While 85% of Londoners find their current housing satisfactory, only 12% of those in our survey reported this...Less than a third of those interviewed had a home big enough for them and their family....45% suffer from disrepair...The way in which this is combined with, and connected to, high levels of unemployment and long-term illness and disability, results in the community feeling demoralised, under attack and sometimes helpless...Housing deprivation is also affecting children's education and chances and intergenerational problems risk young people becoming alienated and involved in crime or anti-social behaviour.'

Why Do Muslims Have Worse Housing Conditions?
Different communities have different housing histories, but we have identified the components of housing disadvantage among many migrant origin communities. Poverty of course plays a part,

and communities that arrived later are less likely to be well housed. Some people however, have been deliberately excluded from housing options. In the 1970s, those arriving from east Africa were 'redlined', excluded from housing waiting lists in some areas, to discourage their settling there.

Key to the better integration of Muslims is a sustained focus on dealing with the causes of housing deprivation.

One London local authority was found to have systematically discriminated against Bangladeshis in the 1980s. Since the 1990s, those seeking asylum are not entitled to mainstream benefits or housing and, since 2000, 'dispersed' to areas of lower housing demand.

What Does Housing Deprivation Have To Do With Integration?

As the Somali report found, people in poor quality or overcrowded housing face considerable barriers to their integration.

- Poor housing conditions are generally associated with high levels of unemployment and underemployment. This is a two-way relationship: obviously low incomes limit housing choices, but poor housing also limits employment options. It makes people ill and managing it takes time and focus that might otherwise be devoted to working or finding work. Some employers discriminate against postcodes where poor housing is prevalent.

- Overcrowding and disrepair militate against learning. Children are less likely to achieve and adults do not have the space or energy to acquire language or other social skills.

- People in poor housing have fewer opportunities for social interaction. Overcrowding may impact local relationships (because of noise and other perceived problems).

So, the key to the better integration of Muslims is a sustained focus on dealing with the causes of housing deprivation. As well as the obvious need to create enough accessible, genuinely affordable and suitable housing for all.

Some mainly Muslim communities (like Somalis and their near

neighbours in north and east London, the Bangladeshi community) also talk of the need for accessible information, trusted advocacy, effective consultation and real engagement.

What About Housing And Segregation?
Since the Cantle report in 2001, there has been concern expressed about the 'segregation' of some communities, almost all identified as Muslim, and often racialised and further stigmatised by anti-migrant rhetoric and Islamophobia.

Within these recent debates segregation has been identified as a problematic choice made by Muslim communities. The evidence however, is that minority ethnic and religious segregation is decreasing and not increasing. Most neighbourhoods are becoming more and not less diverse, including those with large minority ethnic populations.

Table 1
Housing Deprivation by Religion for Muslims and Others from the 2011 Census

	Muslim	Other
White British or Irish	1,283 (33%)	198,763 (9%)
White other	2,411 (38%)	32,252 (28%)
Mixed	1,674 (33%)	11,627 (21%)
Indian	2,505 (26%)	12,385 (21%)
Pakistani	14,603 (29%)	1,417 (30%)
Bangladeshi	8,618 (42%)	892 (41%)
Chinese	167 (41%)	4,826 (27%)
Other Asian	3,453 (36%)	9,766 (31%)
Black African	5,574 (55%)	14,981 (39%)
Black Caribbean	125 (35%)	6,609 (23%)
Black other	1,674 (58%)	3,870 (35%)
Other	5,329 (37%)	4,073 (30%)
Total	**47,416 (35%)**	**301,461 (11%)**

But even if we frame residential segregation as a problem, the question of what causes it is far from clear, and what evidence there is points away from it being the product of a simple choice about preferred neighbours. Most of this looks at ethnicity rather than religion, but as noted above some ethnic groups are primarily Muslim or include large numbers of Muslims.

Research suggests that being able to choose where to live is constrained by income and housing costs, and for ethnic minorities and migrants, by fears of racism. So, any integration policies aimed at Muslims that fail to address the wider issue of the failed housing market and action to reduce and tackle Islamophobia will also fail.

Recommendations

- A sustained focus on dealing with the causes of housing deprivation, address the failed housing market and create enough accessible, genuinely affordable and suitable housing for all.

- Work with Muslim communities to ensure they have accessible information, trusted advocacy, effective consultation and real engagement.

- Find out more about what Muslims and Muslim majority communities believe constrain their housing choices (including fear of Islamophobic and racist hate crimes and harassment) through community supported research.

SUE LUKES

Sue Lukes researches, trains and consults in local services. She teaches migration and housing law and co- edits a website for the Chartered Institute of Housing. As an Industrial Fellow at Manchester University, she is currently working with European cities on how to make migration work for the benefit of all communities involved.

NIGEL DE NORONHA

Dr Nigel de Noronha completed his PhD in Social Statistics at the University of Manchester in 2016 and is a Teaching Fellow at the University of Warwick. He previously worked for the Audit Commission which regulated local government, health and criminal justice agencies as a Performance Auditor.

Tackle Islamophobia Seriously

According to the Cambridge dictionary integration means 'the process of becoming part of a group of people'. Islamophobia is a barrier to integration. It stems from racism to build a stereotypical view of Muslim culture and a false perception of the Islamic mindset that has been generated over the last decade.

I am a Muslim woman with a Pakistani background from Birmingham. These things make me who I am and are a reflection of integration. Yet it is seemingly impossible to express these views without being accused of self-segregation according to the British press.

We need to address the pressing issue of Islamophobia and its increase over the last five years since my father's terrorist murder

Integration and assimilation are two different things. I believe in integrated multiculturalism, which requires respect for everyone regardless of race, religion or class. However, we can only have integration if we reject the politics of hatred and division that are produced by government policy. This has also resulted in the emergence of several far-right racist organisations such as the English Defence League.

My father embodied and reflected what integration meant and because of the British Empire he came to Britain in 1957 to rebuild the country and settled in the West Midlands. He worked in various jobs, which included Aston steel works and eventually worked and retired as a baker. He was also a trade unionist. This country has been nourished and built by immigrants and we must never ever forget that. My father loved and respected this country and the opportunities it gave him and in return my father was a productive and respected member of society.

Muslim Council of Britain

Tragically on the 29th April 2013 my father was stabbed to death by Pavlo Lapshyn, a man known for his racist and neo-Nazi views. My father was murdered for no other reason than the colour of his skin and the religion he followed. Subsequently, Lapshyn went on a three month terrorist bombing campaign and planted bombs outside three mosques in the West Midlands.

Since my father's passing I have been an active campaigner on racism and Islamophobia, standing up to both on a daily basis and speaking and writing on many high-profile platforms.

We need to address the pressing issue of Islamophobia and its increase over the last five years since my father's terrorist murder and the three mosque bombings, much of which has been instigated by right-wing politicians and the mainstream media here in the country. Muslims should be embraced and respected like every other community in an inclusive society. We are human beings just like everyone else. The media has to stop this hate-fuelled reporting and our judiciary needs to review its processes around dealing with cases of hate crime, particularly when there is a sustained targeting of people because of their identity.

Anti-Muslim rhetoric and bigotry have been the main factors for the so called 'War on terror' for over 16 years. And the demonisation of Muslims and Islam has been used to its full extent by the US and UK mainstream media to justify the bombings of Muslim countries. Islamophobia needs to stop and we need to challenge politicians across the globe with their blatant racist rhetoric towards Muslims, migrants and refugees. Muslims are enduring intense discrimination in everyday life at the hands of the media and through government policy.

MAZ SALEEM

Maz Saleem is an anti-war and anti-racist campaigner, a spokesperson for Stand Up To Trump UK and has written for a variety of publications including the Independent. She will be launching an educational website addressing Islamophobia in memory of her father www. efpmohammedsaleem.com for educational purposes and for peace in remembrance of Mohammed Saleem.

Fair Access to Employment

Everyone deserves the opportunity to work without being subjected to harassment or discrimination. Sadly, racism still haunts the British workplace, and black and minority ethnic (BME) workers, including many from Muslim communities, are often singled out for poor treatment.

TUC (Trades Union Congress) research carried out last year[1] found that more than a third of BME workers (37 per cent) had experienced harassment or discrimination. Their experiences ranged from being subject to racist jokes from workmates and physical violence from managers to verbal abuse from members of the public.

One in five (19 per cent) said they had faced discrimination from employers, including being denied training or passed over for promotion.

Many people told our researchers their health had suffered as a result. Almost six out of ten BME women (57 per cent) who had been bullied at work said it affected their mental health. Respondents reported wanting to quit their jobs because of the harassment or discrimination they had suffered – but often said they could not take this risk.

Despite this, many BME workers felt unable to report bullying or discrimination, and those that did were often disappointed by the results. Only 17 per cent of BME workers who have faced discrimination say they reported what happened to their employer, and that it was taken seriously and dealt with satisfactorily.

Racism is often talked about in terms of individual incidents that take place. What the findings show is that there's a problem with workplace culture, and that many BME people are unable to challenge bullying, harassment and discrimination because they lack confidence that their complaints will be listened to.

This creates a toxic environment, which affects not only BME workers, but their families as well. Studies that have analysed the mechanisms linking experiences of discrimination to family members and found that as well as the health impact on the individual it extended to others, including their children's health and development.

> **[We need a strategy] that is not based on the assumption that individual black, ethnic, national and religious minorities workers need to do more to jump over the barriers of discrimination that are erected against them in the workplace.**

The TUC believe that the physical and psychological impacts for BME workers experiencing any form of racism or discrimination or working in a hostile environment are far reaching. It can undermine worker's careers, leave them feeling isolated from colleagues at work and influence relationships with families and friends.

Over the years we have consistently stressed the need for a separate, clear government race equality strategy, and action plan. A strategy that is not based on the assumption that individual black, ethnic, national and religious minorities workers need to do more to jump over the barriers of discrimination that are erected against them in the workplace.

At the TUC we believe this level of inaction to such a serious problem is unacceptable. That's why the right to fair treatment and respect is one of six key elements of our *Great Jobs Agenda*[2] — the blue print for the trade union movement to push employers and politicians to make sure that every worker is paid and treated fairly.

We want employers to work with unions to put in place a zero-tolerance approach to all forms of discrimination, harassment and bullying at work. It's also vital that workers can get justice if they do suffer discrimination, which is why the TUC celebrated the Supreme Court ruling that the introduction of tribunal fees – which resulted in a 79% drop in cases – was unlawful.

The raw deal many BME workers get is just one of the reasons the TUC and unions from across the country supports the rallies against racism and will be marching in London on 12 May in support of a new deal for working people.[3] Because ridding the workplace of racism would be a step towards the more equal and prosperous country our members want.

FRANCES O'GRADY

Frances O'Grady is the General Secretary of the Trades Union Congress (TUC), which brings together 5.5 million working people who make up its 49 member unions. She was previously on the Resolution Foundation's Commission on Living Standards, and has been a member of the Low Pay and the High Pay Commissions.

Notes

1. 1 in 3 British BME workers have been bullied, abused or singled out for unfair treatment, finds TUC poll, TUC, 13 September 2017 <https://www.tuc.org.uk/news/1-3-british-bme-workers-have-been-bullied-abused-or-singled-out-unfair-treatment-finds-tuc-poll>.

2. The Great Jobs Agenda: Giving every worker the opportunity to progress, TUC, 26 June 2017

3. TUC,<https://www.tuc.org.uk/events/new-deal-working-people-tuc-march-rally>

Call Out a Divisive Media

Any policy paper on integration cannot ignore the way that people perceive one another and in particular how British Muslims are viewed by the broader public.

A majority of Brits see Islam as a threat to Western civilisation[1], 37% admitted that they would be more likely to support a political party that promised to reduce the number of Muslims in Britain[2] and the average Brit hugely over-estimates the British Muslim population at three times its actual level.[3] Such a perception is not constrained to adults – even 31% of young children agree that Muslims are taking over England.[4]

Unfortunately, it appears that the majority of the British public (64% according to a YouGov poll)[5] say that what they know about Islam is acquired through the media.

Yet when it comes to sections of the print media in particular, there is a serious and undeniable problem. The United Nations rights chief highlighted the need to tackle UK tabloids' 'vicious verbal assault on migrants & asylum seekers'.[6]

The European Commission considers 'hate speech' to be a serious problem in some traditional media outlets, and worries about it 'fuelling prejudice and showing a reckless disregard' for the dignity and safety of Muslim communities.[7] Academic studies support international observations, whether it is the University of Cambridge talking about mainstream media reporting about Muslims contributing to an 'atmosphere of rising hostility' towards Muslims or the University of Leicester experts, who say 'politicians and media fuel hate crime in Britain'.

Through work over the past year and a half, over 50 instances of pure and simple false stories about Islam and Muslims have been corrected after complaints I have personally made – not far off one a week!

Such inaccuracies were the reason why the Guardian published a piece entitled 'Press publishing 'consistent stream' of inaccurate stories about Muslims' just over a year ago.

Examples of false and hate-filled stories about Muslims, many of which have been shared by far-right extremists as well as contributed to creating and shaping the narrative about British Muslims, include:

- 'Christian child forced into Muslim foster care' (Andrew Norfolk, front page of *The Times* for 4 days, August 2017); also on the front page of *The Daily Mail*.

- Nazi-like language about Muslims 'What will we do about The Muslim Problem then?' (Trevor Kavanagh, *The Sun,* August 2017).

- Belittling the ethnic cleansing of Rohingya Muslims in Myanmar (Rod Liddle, *The Sun*, September 2017).

- 'Islamists may have already infiltrated our armed forces' (Richard Kemp, *The Times*, August 2017).

- 'Dawa: the Islamist mind poison that turns lost souls into 'lone wolves'' (Niall Ferguson, *The Times*, March 2017).

- Andrew Gilligan:
    - Falsely claiming 'Enclaves of Islam see UK as 75% Muslim' (*The Times,* December 2016)
    - Falsely accusing Mr Haras Ahmed of being an 'Islamist activist' (*The Telegraph,* apology in August 2017)
    - Falsely claiming that Mohammed Kozbar 'blamed the UK for Isil' (*The Telegraph*, apology in September 2016)
    - Falsely claiming Mrs Smith is a member of or affiliated to the Musllim Brotherhood or an Islamic extremist (*The Telegraph,* apology in October 2016)
    - Falsely claiming Mr Mujibul Islam was 'a willing beneficiary of... corruption' (*The Telegraph,* apology in May 2016)

- '...if we want peace then we need one thing – less Islam' (Douglas Murray, *The Sun,* June 2017).

This list excludes a host of other stories that build up a dangerous narrative about Muslim communities e.g. The Telegraph and Sunday Times apologised for claiming two Muslims were responsible for a 'Trojan Horse' plot in Oldham; and it excludes the problems (albeit less frequent) within broadcast media e.g. Douglas Murray was given an unchallenged platform on the BBC Sunday Politics to spout a false, misleading and hate-filled diatribe about Muslims, reiterating his unjustifiable claim that less Islam leads to less terrorism.

Even those articles where the newspapers acknowledged their error did not have corrections of equal prominence, nor did they undo the damage already caused.

With these serious problems within sections of print media and even broadcast media leading to such a plethora of inaccurate stories, and hate-filled and scaremongering opinion pieces about Islam and Muslims, there is little wonder that we see such an appalling perception of Muslim communities.

Irresponsible reporting not only affects British Muslims – it affects the trust that the British public has with the media.

Such irresponsible reporting not only affects British Muslims – it affects the trust that the British public has with the fantastic reporters that day-in day-out, provide important stories which challenge authority and speak truth to power.

And the main press regulator IPSO struggles with its independence, has huge deficiencies in the rules it sets out (no protection for groups such as Muslims, no requirement for equal prominence for corrections to articles) and has thus far failed to institute a single fine for a breach of standards within the media or even investigate racism or Islamophobia.

We need a strong and responsible media that reports the truth – and does not castigate minorities. How can we have an integration strategy without addressing one the key drivers of hate that tear communities apart?

Recommendations
- Show leadership e.g. politicians publicly making statements against Islamophobia within the press.

- Encourage and improve diversity within all sections and levels of media: from journalists up to editors, producers and decision-makers.

- Develop religious literacy across media outlets to decrease the malicious agenda-driven anti-Muslim articles.

- Improve the regulatory process given the identified problems with the self-regulatory process headed by IPSO through the implementation of Lord Leveson's recommendations, including Section 40 of the Crime and Courts Act 2013 and 'Leveson 2'.

- Strengthen freedom of speech by media outlets giving space to minority communities to respond to hate-filled opinion writers.

- Request social media outlets to require media publishers to follow a Code of Practice, whereby corrections to inaccuracies reach the same users who saw the initial false articles.

MIQDAAD VERSI

Miqdaad Versi is Assistant Secretary General of the Muslim Council of Britain. He is most renowned for his work tackling media misreporting, having elicited over 50 corrections from national press and was named by the BBC as "The man correcting stories on Muslims".

Notes

1. 7/7 Bombings Anniversary Poll Shows More Than Half Of Britons See Muslims As A Threat, Huffington Post, July 2015

2. Voters more likely to back an anti-Muslim party than reject it – poll, Guardian, September 2012

3. Perceptions are not reality: what the world gets wrong, Ipsos Mori, December 2016

4. Racist and anti-immigration views held by children revealed in schools study, Guardian, May 2015

5. Attitudes towards British Muslims, YouGov, November 2002

6. Statement by UN High Commissioner for Human Rights, Zeid Ra'ad Al Hussein, April 2015

7. ECRI Report on the United Kingdom (5th monitoring cycle), European Commission against Racism and Intolerance, October 2016

The Art and Culture of Challenging Islamophobia

In her work on justice and difference the American political theorist Iris Marion Young identifies the 'fives faces of oppression' encountered by disadvantaged social groups. She names these as exploitation, marginalisation, powerlessness, violence and cultural imperialism. The first three refer to structural and institutional relations that shape their material lives and the fourth to threats and dangers to physical safety. The last of these, a form of cultural theft, exclusion and oppression, occurs when 'the dominant meanings of society render the particular perspective of one's own group invisible at the same time as they stereotype one's own group and mark it out as Other'. At once invisible and hyper-visible. The invisibility, Young notes, 'comes from when the dominant group fails to recognise the perspective embodied in their cultural expression as a perspective' and difference is 'reconstructed largely as deviance and inferiority', a sign of something lacking.

Young's notion of cultural oppression captures the experiences felt by many Muslims in Britain. While there is more discussion around Muslims today than ever before in government, the media and cultural spaces across Britain and abroad, they are almost exclusively focused on issues of radicalisation and otherness and often fail to engage, challenge or empower the communities they seek to analyse in terms of their arts and cultural heritage. Reflecting the scale and intensity of negative news coverage, Muslim activists and civil society organisation have focused much of their attention on print and broadcast news media, calling out and challenging inaccuracies and stereotyping and drawing attention to facts and data. As if fear, prejudice and Islamophobia can be overcome with better facts or better evidence alone.

A second response has been to note the potential for art and culture to shape the public conversation and challenge stereotypes; not through new hard facts and better data, but through captivating stories, images and narratives that engage people's senses, empathy and emotions. But there is a risk here of staying within an agenda shaped and defined by the need to disprove the dominant meaning ascribed to Muslims. It means addressing the questions that are asked of you, rather than exploring the questions you want answers to. It reinforces a system, in which Britain's approximately three million Muslims are rarely seen or heard on mainstream platforms discussing philosophy, science, literature or the arts in multi-faith and non-faith contexts. Diversity within Muslim communities, the plurality of Muslim cultures and the richness of their artistic traditions, thus remain grossly under-represented.

Diversity within Muslim communities, the plurality of Muslim cultures and the richness of their artistic traditions, thus remain grossly under-represented.

A third response is for Muslims, through writing, art and performance, to explore the issues and experiences that are important to them and are shaping their lives. This was in large part, the motivation behind MFest, the festival of Muslim cultures and ideas which will take place at the British Library in April 2018. Over two and a half days it creates space to explore issues ranging from the role of artificial intelligence and algorithms in shaping knowledge and identities — including knowledge about Muslims and Islam — through to futures and alternative worlds imagined by Muslim sci-fi writers. There will be panels on the future of Muslim activism, the Caribbean Ummah and the evolution of feminisms. It brings together leading writers, thinkers and artists and art practitioners who will facilitate the exploration of Muslim identity in a way that prioritises the needs of Muslims themselves.

While the festival does not aim to challenge Islamophobia directly, through discussion and workshops on poetry, comic book creation and zine making, MFest will give communities and individuals the chance to investigate the questions that they want answers to. It creates space for the expression and exploration of the diversity of Muslim cultural and artistic traditions and undermines an Islamophobia that sees Muslims as a static and monolithic block.

The growth and development of this diversity, requires access to the means of cultural production and avenues for the dissemination of their work. This remains a daunting task when the cultural institutions and creative industries have far to go to reflect the diversity of modern Britain.

Demographic and technology changes are beginning to restructure parts of the old cultural landscape, creating new ways for writers, artists, performers to engage and reach their audiences, exchange ideas and tell their stories. For example, in the last two years we have seen major publishers Simon and Schuster establish Salaam Reads, as an imprint for books targeted at young Muslim readers. At the same time, new BME led publishers like Jacaranda Books and Knights Of have established themselves with the aim of publishing books with stories and characters that reflect the diversity of modern British society. Their existence highlights the role that Muslim communities can play in arts and cultural production. By recognising the arts and creative expression as a legitimate part of what it means to be a Muslim and encouraging and supporting artists and those who want to pursue arts careers, we help ensure that our particular perspectives are visible and relevant.

NAIMA KHAN

Naima Khan has a background in arts journalism with specialisms in theatre and film and has worked in radio and third sector communications. She is the Programme Manager for MFest, Arts & Culture Officer at the Aziz Foundation, Social Media Coordinator for TEDxLondon and a trustee of the Inclusive Mosque Initiative.

TUFYAL CHOUDHURY

Tufyal Choudhury is Director of MFest. He is an Assistant Professor of Law at Durham University researching issues of inclusion and integration of Muslim communities in Europe and North America.

Participating in Public Life

At Citizens UK, we are celebrating our 30th Anniversary this year. We also marked the 20th Anniversary of our first Citizens Alliance in London (The East London Citizens Alliance; TELCO) last year. This event particularly illustrated the distinctive nature of our work which is to build permanent self-funding diverse Alliances of powerful local civil society institutions that stay and organise together for the common good. One of the largest and most impressive founding member institutions is the East London Mosque in Whitechapel. A very early (in 1997) successful campaign of Citizens UK, was to stand and organise together, negotiate with the local Council and a major developer to release the privately owned land adjacent to the Mosque, to be used to build the London Muslim Centre. Since that time the 50 plus member groups of TELCO have been involved in hundreds of local, regional and even national campaigns to tackle a range of injustices, whilst also training a new generation of civic leaders on how to 'organise' more effectively in the 21st century.

However Citizens UK is not first and foremost a campaigning organisation. Our charitable objective is 'to support and enhance the capacity of the people of the UK to participate in public life and to strengthen the groups they come from in the process'. This important point is missed by the pundits and others who only know us for our multi-issue list of campaigns and causes. We help strengthen local rooted institutions like mosques, schools and refugee groups by sharing the tools of community organising and thus enhancing the democratic process and development of civic leaders for the future. By joining a Citizens Alliance, local groups also learn how to be more powerful by being in a relationship and acting together on issues and concerns that are shared. This serves to enhance integration and strengthen community ties.

In 2015 our UK membership Council, supported by Citizens Trustees initiated the 'Citizens Commission on Islam, Participation and Public Life'. This was chaired by the Rt Hon Dominic Grieve MP and included a diverse group of senior business, military and civic leaders. The aim of this Commission was partly to celebrate the many excellent examples of participation and leadership by UK Muslim Communities, but nevertheless to also consider the root causes of why, over the last ten years, many British Muslims have felt they could not participate or were not being encouraged to participate in public life.

The stimulus for what has become known as the 'Missing Muslims Report', was partly a major negative shift in the dominant narrative of the media and public officials, but also Citizens' own growing experience on the streets of the UK's major cities, where the recruitment of mosques and Muslim groups into a diverse Citizens Alliance was once relatively easy, had now become more difficult, and the leadership of such institutions more anxious about the welcome they would receive.

The outcome of two years of work by the Commission, alongside hundreds of testimonies, both positive and negative stories about 'participation' and what it is like to be a Muslim in the UK today is a major report which I commend to the reader. Partly because it is full of positive stories and practical solutions, but also because it is not primarily addressed to the UK government but to Civil Society-ourselves. 30 years of organising across the UK has taught us that many of the solutions to the challenges we face can be found locally, and that by working together with like-minded groups, we do have the power to change and challenge the systems which prevent our right to participate and help shape our shared destiny.

Apart from reading and acting on the 'Missing Muslims' Commission Report and noting the many inspirational examples of communities and groups of individuals already acting together to strengthen society, I offer three specific actions for you to consider:

1. **Take a lead on the new opportunity to 'Sponsor Syrian Refugee Families'.** This initiative is only available for registered charities in the UK – like mosques or Muslim institutions. It involves raising £10k; finding and furnishing a house; building a team; being accredited as a sponsor by the Home Office – and then going to your local airport to welcome the family (identified by UNHCR from the thousands of refugees stranded in the camps around Syria). This major challenge to civil society has been mainstream in Canada for the last 40 years and led to thousands of refugees

moving to Canada and being welcomed and quickly integrated into local communities. Contact Citizens 'Sponsor Refugees Foundation' for more information at www.sponsorrefugees.org.

2. **Act together with neighbouring institutions to ensure that housing near to your institution remains permanently affordable into the future through Community Land Trusts.** The fight for land to house and keep low and moderate income families together and near the civic institutions they/we create is ancient and historic. A mosque cannot just be a worship centre and watch the local Muslim community be slowly squeezed out of the neighbourhood by rising costs and market forces leaving the mosque like a stranded whale when the tide goes out. To challenge the dominance of the developers and speculators, every mosque should have an ongoing campaign to ensure that the families served do not have to move, put their roots down and stay together across the generations. Contact London Community Land Trust for more information.

3. **If there is a Citizens UK Alliance in your area ensure that the mosque or group you attend joins it, if not build one!** There is strength, experience, intelligence, solidarity, protection and power in permanent diverse alliances made up of rooted civic institutions that fund themselves and employ their own organiser to train, support and encourage them to play their rightful part in a vibrant democracy.

NEIL JAMESON

Neil Jameson is the Founding Executive Director of Citizens UK. Neil has been named by *The Guardian* as one of the UK's most significant public servants. In 2012, he was made an Honorary Fellow of Queen Mary London University. He was awarded a CBE in 2016 in recognition of his services to the community and social justice.

Activism as Integration

We all have multiple identities — ethnic or racial, faith or no faith. They are complementary, not competitive. The multiplicity of our identities – our human diversity, or pluralism in a society — is a matter of celebration. We all are equal, but different. In Islam, the concept of human diversity is very positive — as human beings are born individuals and not clones to one another. Human diversity is like a garden that comprises of multi-coloured flowers — people from different colours, shapes and styles.

Diversity by its nature can bring natural differences and dissension. Each of us has our unique features, strengths and weaknesses. But together we are better. The big test for us is to prove whether our differences create synergy and bring with them peace, or pit one against another to make the planet uninhabitable.

Building bridges among people in neighbourhoods and creating good community relations are at the heart of Islam's social life. Muslims are expected to excel in qualities of tolerance and respect in order to create a safer and better community and society. Despair, alienation and grievances should not lead them to adopt policies and actions that go against religious principles and public interest. Muslims are reminded by the teachings of Islam to rise above the challenges thrown at them or against their religion, especially in the post-9/11 world. They should be at the forefront of serving all in society – unilaterally and without expecting any favour or return. That is what morally upright Muslims are commanded to do. This starts in one's neighbourhood — irrespective of people's backgrounds.

We all have obligations to help fellow human beings, passing on good wishes to our neighbours in their good fortune, sharing food when cooked on special occasions, visiting and helping when they are ill or in distress, and attending their funeral when they die. Neighbours deserve not to be harmed or harassed in any way.

With Islam's inherent community spirit, Muslims should perform better with inclusive multiple identities: they do not only have to be Muslim-centric, or focus only on their ethnic or cultural identity. Muslims should never have an identity crisis; they can be British, be it Bradfordian or Brummie, and Muslim in the same way. This is the best way to defeat extremism, bigotry and 'othering'. Islam teaches that duty towards others as well as to our planet is unconditional and unilateral.

> *If Muslim organisations wish to contribute to Britain's cultural and political life, that is not only their right but their patriotic duty.*

Diversity without a robust equality of opportunity is meaningless. It ends up dividing people, not uniting them. The House of Commons Women and Equalities Select Committee (WESC), in its report on Employment opportunities for Muslims in the UK in August 2016, reported that 'Muslim people suffer the greatest economic disadvantages of any group in society'. With unemployment rates more than twice those of the general population, the community's economic woes are far greater.

With a significantly larger youth population compared to wider society the community has a huge potential to perform better. While the community's success in the education sector has been enviable in the past two decades, its social mobility is still very weak due to structural, internal and external factors. Civil society and the business sector can offer their helping hands to take down the barriers such as higher unemployment and the glass ceiling that young Muslims are facing in the job market.

In a great society like Britain's, diversity is an asset that promotes positive integration and negates isolation, segregation or insularity. Pluralism paves the way for a richer culture that is open, non-combative and celebratory. If people from diverse backgrounds across the UK self-identify as a religious community, that is their right. If they set up organisations that defend their ethnic interests, that is their right.

If Muslim organisations wish to contribute to Britain's cultural and political life, that is not only their right but their patriotic duty. In an age when so many powerful people are corrupt or out of touch with ordinary people, disseminating public duty ethically is vital.

Islam's teaching is not to be judgmental. The Qur'an demands from the believers to 'repel evil with what is better....' (Qur'an 23:96). Muslims are supposed to be a middle-path community treading the 'middle way' (*Wasatiyya* in Arabic) of life. While Islam accommodates radical ideas, it detests extremism; the Qur'an mentions '.... do not commit excess in your religion' (Qur'an 4:171, 5:77).

The Prophet as an exemplar to Muslims advised and practised moderation in life. He asked believers to achieve the best of human character by saying 'I have only been sent to perfect good moral character' (Prophetic Hadith, Musnad Ahmad). We should follow the Prophet's example in our civic engagements to contribute toward building a better Britain.

Mosques are primarily places of worship in the Islamic faith with an estimated 1,750 mosques across the UK serving Britain's three million Muslims and their local communities.

However, mosques are seen by some as threatening, dangerous and undesirable, fuelled by anti-Muslim rhetoric in the media and fear-mongering from right-wing campaigners.

MUHAMMAD ABDUL BARI

Dr Muhammad Abdul Bari MBE is a community activist and educationalist. He has served in leadership positions in the Muslim community including as Secretary General of the Muslim Council of Britain and chair of the East London Mosque Trust. He was awarded a MBE in the 2003 New Year's Honours List.

Section Four

Muslims Integral to Our National Story

Do Muslims Lead Separate Lives?

Travelling around Muslim Britain, as I did throughout 2016, it doesn't take long to appreciate how mixed and complex the story on Muslim 'integration' really is. Some communities are demonstrably thriving on new diversity. The energy and vibrancy it brings is plain for all to see in east London, say, or central Manchester. Some 200 languages are spoken in that city, making it perhaps the most linguistically diverse in the world - a fact of which many Mancunians are rightly proud. And yet, ten miles to the north east, I visited Glodwick in Oldham, an area heavily dominated by British Pakistanis, and the area worst affected in the Oldham race riot of 2001 — a riot that Professor Ted Cantle, the noted expert on social cohesion who reported on it for the government, blamed largely on years of racial segregation in the town. The segregation persists today and Glodwick is not alone: I saw similar symbols of the failure of the integration project in many other English towns.

Where does this mutual suspicion and distrust come from? How and why do neighbours become and remain so aggressively segregated? Oldham has taken some innovative steps to try to reverse the process. In 2010, for instance, it set up Waterhead Academy, an integrated school deliberately formed from the merger of two others, the predominantly Asian Breeze Hill School and a predominantly white one, Counthill. Yet the reality of Glodwick perhaps proves how resistant people can be to such social engineering.

It is, of course, only human to want to live among people of one's own background. In Dewsbury in Yorkshire, with its virtually mono-ethnic Asian Muslim suburb of Savile Town, I learned that urban segregation is a two-way process. Savile Town was formed not only by new arrivals clustering, but also by native whites departing: the well-documented phenomenon of 'white flight.' The social consequences can be dire, and nowhere more so than in Dewsbury. The town centre of this ancient town has been catastrophically hollowed out. Shops, pubs and municipal offices are boarded up,

The Birmingham Central Mosque. Birmingham is home to one of the largest Muslim communities in the UK.

and a big Victorian church has been converted into a mosque. The white middle classes have fled, leaving behind an impoverished white underclass struggling with drugs and crime. The town also has an unenviable reputation for racial tension — as well as for producing terrorists. 'There's just this feeling that white sensitivities have been abandoned by a liberal elite,' said a retired [white] Dewsbury policeman, who had himself moved out to the nearby suburb of Mirfield.

Can white flight be stemmed, or put into reverse? Professor Cantle thinks so.

'Politicians and policymakers need to encourage white British residents to remain in diverse areas; to choose, rather than avoid, diverse areas when they do relocate,' he said in 2016. 'We've never sold the idea that mixed communities are more exciting places to live, with more going on.' That is not, however, a message that has yet gained much traction in Dewsbury.

Another startlingly altered locale is east Birmingham, the heart of a Muslim community 250,000-strong, where I investigated an alleged Islamist plot — the so-called 'Trojan horse' plot, later shown to be non-existent — to 'take over' several of the area's state schools.

> *It is not enough merely to recognise the obvious fact that integration is a two-way street.*

Tahir Alam, a senior educationalist and the alleged ringleader of the plot, was subsequently banned for life from any further role in the education system. Alam, however, argued (and still argues) that, given the make-up of the catchment areas served by those state schools, there is nothing wrong with running them according to 'an Islamic ethos' - especially when, as was the case with his schools, they were such conspicuously successful ones academically. Of the 14 state schools caught up in the Trojan Horse affair, all of which are within five miles of each other, not one had an ethnic minority pupil intake of less than 96 per cent. Is Muslim culture a part of modern British society, or not? The question was being asked once again this January following a row surrounding children's hijabs at a primary school in Newham in east London.

Muslim culture, along with its traditions (such as sharia law) and outward tropes (such as hijabs or niqabs) are sometimes grotesquely misunderstood by non-Muslims — and more could and should be done to correct those misperceptions through public education. Initiatives like the Muslim Council of Britain's annual 'Visit My Mosque' day do much to break down prejudices, and deserve all the official support they can get. The media, too, has a vital role to play.

For too long, sections of the tabloid (and not so tabloid) press have stoked prejudice and fear through lazy, sensationalist or downright malicious reporting. The rhetoric about, for instance, Muslim 'no-go zones' in British cities, most notoriously propagated by Fox News, needs constant rebuttal. Needless to say, on my travels in the country, I found not one Muslim-majority community where I did not feel safe, and welcome. The paradox of segregated communities is that while they may appear threatening to outsiders — and indeed, to the government — they are often pleasant places in which to live.

All this said, it is wrong to place all the blame for the failure of integration on non-Muslims. Some Muslims, too, need to be more pro-active in the way that they interact with their neighbours. In Birmingham's Alum Rock, I interviewed an 11-year-old Asian Muslim who attended Hamdh House, a small private faith school of 150 pupils. His father, an IT consultant from Reading, had moved to Birmingham because the religious schooling opportunities were better; he was highly educated, civic-minded, and deeply engaged in his community through the local mosque. The son was into park football, but when I asked who he played with, it emerged that not only were there no non-Muslims on his team, but also that he knew no non-Muslims whatsoever.

It is not enough merely to recognise the obvious fact that integration is a two-way street. For it to succeed in practice also requires will, vigilant self-appraisal, and hard work, even — indeed, perhaps particularly — within the private sphere of the family.

JAMES FERGUSSON

James Fergusson is a freelance journalist and foreign correspondent who has written for many publications including the *Independent*, *The Times*, the *Daily Mail* and *The Economist*. He is the author of *Al-Britannia, My Country: A Journey through Muslim Britain*.

Remember our Forgotten Heroes

For almost a century, the true extent of the contribution of Muslim soldiers and labourers, who served alongside the Allies in the First World War, has been largely unknown, and remains so. Unfortunately, this lack of knowledge has led to narrow, inaccurate recollections of the diversity in the Great War, resulting in mostly European-centric commemorations in public life, in history books, in classroom materials, and of course in television, film and news media.

Furthermore, this has also led to many being suspicious of the reasons why this information has been 'forgotten'. Some might say that it is part of a 'cover-up' of how European nations betrayed colonial troops; or how they were treated as second-class and subjected to racism, while they were being led to the battlefields like lambs to the slaughter. Others might say that they were forced to enlist and used as cannon fodder. Unfortunately, those who may believe these theories have accepted them as being true without evidence or having any real knowledge or understanding on the subject. Maybe some will continue to believe that, but without learning what we have discovered, these views don't consider the whole picture.

In summary, First World War story-telling is inaccurate and resulting attitudes are unhelpful barriers to learning the truth. Allow me to address some of those views by offering a common-sense view.

First of all, while there was forced enlistment by some units, the majority of Muslim soldiers and labourers from around the world enlisted by their own free will. Let's be honest: recruitment was done in a panic but it offered paid employment, and colonial troops had families to feed at home in undeveloped nations. More credit to them – they came to the aid of Europe when they didn't have to therefore, are deserving of the respect of Europeans for that fact alone.

Secondly, we have not found any evidence of racism, xenophobia

or sectarianism in our research. In fact, it is the opposite: many Muslim soldiers were respected by their Christian, Jewish, Hindu, Sikh, Zoroastrian and other brothers-in-arms. They all mutually respected and admired one another and went to great lengths to look out for each other. Many Muslim soldiers were more decorated than their European counterparts and the respect shown to the Algerian Spahis came from the top. King George V visited the battlefields and broke with protocol to humble himself by dismounting his horse in their presence.

Thirdly, everyone was cannon-fodder. It was a bloody war fought in small battlegrounds that resulted in the estimated deaths of over 18,500,000 people.

First World War story-telling is inaccurate and resulting attitudes are unhelpful barriers to learning the truth.

So what have Forgotten Heroes 14-19 Foundation uncovered, and how? To put it simply: we located 850,000 original documents which is real evidence concerning over 2,500,000 Muslim soldiers and labourers who served with the Allies, specifically by seeking documents in Arabic, Farsi, Hebrew, Urdu, Hindi, Punjabi, Gujarati, etc.

Muslim Council of Britain

Was there a cover-up? Of course not. In my view, these documents were 'forgotten' because, as custodians of war records withdrew at the end of the War, it wasn't a priority to translate and index all of these documents, and very few personnel in Europe spoke those languages. So we opened these documents for the first time after nearly 100 years.

War is never pretty and has tragic consequences. But this project is not making judgment on the politics of war nor military strategy. Nor is this project an endorsement of colonialism, or a recruitment tool. It is simply to acknowledge, and pay tribute to, millions of Muslims who were there but are not recognised; to celebrate diversity and our shared heritage; and apply the lessons of mutual respect and tolerance that colonial people of all different backgrounds and faiths championed with their brothers-in-arms from 1914-1919; the Centenary of their contribution doesn't end for them until 2019.

We also believe that our research can lead to a more accurate understanding and teaching of the Great War, which can challenge Islamophobia and far-right extremists who deny the contribution that Muslims have made to the history and security of Europe. Teaching this will improve social cohesion and how we reject xenophobia, and talk about the integration and acceptance of minorities.

As the world commemorates the First World War Centenary in November 2018, now is the moment to recognise these Forgotten Heroes.

Do you want to improve the narrative of how Muslims are known in today's world?

HAYYAN BHABHA

Hayyan is Executive Director of MuslimsinWW1. com – an archival project of Forgotten Heroes 14-19 Foundation, an independent Belgian NGO funded only by donations. Hayyan is also an Independent Member of the Anti-Muslim Hatred Working Group; and Co-Founder and Former Secretary of the APPG on British Muslims.

Face Up to Our Colonial Past

From the textile mills of West Yorkshire, to the Notting Hill Carnival in West London, the Curry Mile in Manchester and Bangla Town in Tower Hamlets to the clusters of Somali and Yemeni restaurants in Shepherds Bush, immigration defines and re-defines the cultural milieu of Britishness today. These communities which arrived from ex-colonies after the British Nationality Act of 1948 also connect Britain to its past.

Colonialism is an inescapable legacy of this migration. It is deeply tied to the diversity of faith, background and race of Britain in the same ways Senegalese, Algerian, Moroccan, Malian and other communities define the ethnic make up of France. But when the topic of integration is raised, it's summed up by a need to solve the inalienable question of 'integrating' immigrants or Muslims.

In 2016, The Casey Review sought to examine opportunity and integration in the most 'deprived and isolated' parts of Britain. Its conclusions stuck to the script of removing any discussions of historical context. Instead, Dame Louise Casey chose to pinpoint 'council wards of 85% from a single minority background' consisting of 'deprived Pakistani or Bangladeshi cultures.' In an article in *The Guardian*, Casey argued that 'retreat' and 'retrenchment sometimes go hand in hand with deeply regressive religious and cultural practices.'

Casey's comments draw striking resemblance to the words of colonialist, Thomas Babington Macaulay who echoed a similar mantra. In 1835, he delivered a speech entitled 'A Minute on Education' in reference to British India where Macaulay affirmed the need to create a 'class of persons Indian in colour but English in tastes, in opinions, in morals and in intellect.' Crucially, he went on to describe the need to draw from 'Western nomenclature.'

Macaulay's statements were seminal because they provided the framework for what 'becoming British' would look like. His particular vision was about desecrating anything distinctly Indian from literature, to language to traditions. These colonial norms sowed the seeds for the kinds of discourse we have today around integration albeit using more coded language. But the prevalence of these norms go way beyond language.

Today, our concepts of citizenship tests and naturalisation processes arbitrarily decide when a 'foreigner' becomes 'British.' Similarly, Macauley's vision of stopping the printing of 'Arabic and Sanskrit books' in British India is strikingly similar to the Government's cultural anxiety around the cultures of immigrants, people of colour and Muslims whose practices are 'deeply regressive' as Louise Casey identified. Integration in this context is drawn from colonial thinking which is defined by shedding your rich traditions and becoming the good native, or, to use the title of the book and collection of essays by writers of colour in Britain and edited by Nikesh Shukla, 'The Good Immigrant'.

The good immigrant is therefore uncritical of government, wins Olympic Gold and is perpetually grateful. Whereas the bad immigrant is the rapper who dares to critique the state and wears their culture on their chest.

These falsehoods centre on the logic that minority communities, Muslims and immigrants contribute a self-segregated Britain.

The discourse around integration and the prevailing discussions which centre on Muslims, minorities and immigrants clearly have a narrow scope, but the debates are also subject to myth-making. These falsehoods centre on the logic that minority communities, Muslims and immigrants contribute to a self-segregated Britain. This mirage of 'choice' is parroted across the mainstream media and in political discussions.

Communities which migrated from former colonies, from the West Indies to South Asian communities, arrived in Britain throughout the 50s/60s/70s and 80s at a time when structural and physical racism was an enduring reality. In an era of Enoch Powell, the National Front and where signs like 'No Dogs, No blacks, No Irish' were commonplace. These immigrants were settling in a country where racist housing policies existed, where 'white flight' was prevalent and physical racism was rife. It's no surprise then, that communities settled in protective clusters, not of choice, but out of necessity. The Migration Observatory based at the University of Oxford noted that 'the presence of immigrant communities can also help migrants to cope with personal and cultural stress associated with migration' and where fellow immigrants provide support with jobs, housing and child care.

The debate around integration assumes that everyone starts at the same point. How far people get in society is measured by the willingness to 'integrate' and work hard. But this does not take into consideration the historical legacies of where Muslims, immigrants and minority, ethnic communities have come from. Projects like Our Migration Story, a collaboration between the Runnymede Trust and academics at the universities of Cambridge and Manchester provide insight into Britain's longstanding history with migrant communities from 1500s to the present day. These untold stories redress the balance and provide first-hand examples of what Britishness truly looks like, historically and in the present.

MOHAMED-ZAIN DADA

Mohamed-Zain Dada is a producer at the Free Word Centre and has a BA in Politics and History at SOAS, University of London. Zain is the co-founder of Decolonising Our Minds Society. He is also the co-director of Khidr Collective, a multi-disciplinary arts collective supporting the work of young British, Muslim artists from across the UK.

Section Five
Muslim Perspectives

A Convert Muslim Experience

There are many challenges of identity for converts to Islam e.g. how to reconcile and amalgamate one's Islamic identity and one's former identity. This is further frustrated by the culturally infused Islam which is part and parcel of many Muslim communities.

Why does everything have to change as a result of conversion? We may have taken a step back to our natural *fitra* (state of being), our social circle may have expanded, but we are essentially the same person, albeit with a transformed outlook of the world. This imposition faced by many converts, has to stop and Muslim communities have to allow the convert community to provide the culturally sensitive and mature leadership required for their own community.

Very few converts are fortunate in their families embracing and accepting the change. Exposure to Islam brings with it an anxiety that is passed on to the convert who is already dealing with this new direction in life, but has to now cope with the pressure from those closest to them. The non-Muslim family in turn fear losing their family member and understandably fear the unknown.

A strong British Muslim heritage, especially a convert Muslim heritage needs to be cultivated so that a sense of belonging is deeply rooted into the Muslim psyche here in Britain. We have a long way to go before we see a truly British expression of Islam.

Converts are not recognised or respected as a legitimate community. We are not being empowered to address our own concerns and to take our development forward in our own right. This is certainly a challenge for the convert community; we need to develop a structure of training that will empower us and enable us to take positions of authority and leadership in the wider Muslim community. We have growing groups of scholars and activists but no recognition. We have no social capital and are very much marginalised within the community. The existing Muslim community need to create spaces to allow for this to happen.

Da'wah (propagation) through action is the way forward. When people see our neighbourhoods as they should be seen they will come to the mosques and respect us. Mosques engaging in communities need to realise that they have to work much harder in engaging internally with themselves before we can make this move outwards. We need to have better integration between different Muslim groups and in the community as a whole.

Interacting in the workplace as a Muslim brings positive responses; it interests people and is an excellent platform from which things can be discussed in a polite and interesting manner. Organisations like St Phillips, One Roof, Help the Homeless in Leicester, churches and City Circle do a wonderful job of bringing together like-minded people and working together to improve the general wellbeing of society.

It is only through social interaction and establishing social programmes and projects which benefit all communities, that we will be able us to interact with the rest of society and change attitudes by our behaviour and our generosity of spirit and professionalism.

We need to arrive at a real understanding of the cultural landscape in which we are living. If we want to engage with society we need to know what goes on in the quiet landscapes of the UK. Converts to Islam were not raised in the gutter nor raised with thieves and the fact that they have come to Islam does not mean that they have come straight from hell into the civilised Muslim community. The great majority come from loving homes and it is to these families and homes they eventually turn back to for comfort when they are feeling isolated from the Muslim community. Muslim communities must understand that cultural sensitivity works both ways – It must be expressed towards converts in terms of their own cultural elements.

BATOOL AL-TOMA

Batool Al-Toma is Director of the New Muslims Project, a UK-based service supporting converts to Islam. She is the UK representative for the European Muslim Network (EMN) thinktank in Brussels.

Muslim Women's Perspectives

A cursory glance at statistics involving gender-based violence, representation of women in public life and access to employment and services will demonstrate that misogyny and sexism exist in every culture and community in the UK. It's clear that no one community is responsible for these behaviours more than any other.

It is also true that there are different norms and beliefs that dictate how individuals and communities respond to societal challenges. While sexism is expressed differently according to socio-economic, environmental or cultural factors, these expressions generally come from the same basis, and it is this basis that we can focus on tackling.

So where do Muslims stand? Integration is a complex issue and treatment of women is often cited and fiercely debated. There are both internal and external factors to consider. On one hand, we're confronted by sections who vehemently deny any wrongdoing and contest the very existence of sexism. On the other, you have a minority of well-intentioned men who do want to encourage progression and break this cycle of silence but are completely dumbfounded as to where we should begin. One has to ask: why is it the case that Muslim communities are so reluctant to confront this issue head-on?

For those of us born and raised in the UK, the answer is quite simple and something we are fairly familiar with; in a climate of rampant Islamophobia, there is a perception that internal 'divisions' will be exploited, weaponised against us and used as justification for Islamophobia.

Muslim women sit at the heart of this debate. Our experiences are tokenised and used as definitive proof that Islam and Muslims are at odds with 'British values' and, by extension, the state. To demonstrate the extent to which this can be taken, one only need look to the war in Afghanistan to note that concern about women's rights can serve as a façade for war-mongering policies.

For many people, a fundamental premise of the integration debate is that Muslim women, by virtue of our identity and religious expression, are oppressed.

For many people, a fundamental premise of the integration debate is that Muslim women, by virtue of our identity and religious expression, are oppressed. The tired orientalist trope is alive and well — that we are controlled and subjugated by Muslim men, simultaneously hypersexualised and sexually repressed, and often spoken about in terms of unveiling or liberating. There's an entire genre of literature dedicated to the 'unveiling' (read: what's 'behind', 'beneath' and 'under' the veil) of Muslim women. When you combine this with an unhealthy political obsession with hijabs and niqabs in public life, one begins to understand that mainstream British society has yet to get 'beyond' the veil and its various associated metaphors.

Muslim women are thus placed in an uncomfortable position — one that Mona Eltahawy describes as 'a rock and a hard place': between racists who want to demonise all Muslim men and a community that wants to defend and absolve all Muslim men.

This exemplifies the crux of the issue(s) facing Muslim women today: Muslim women continue to be seen as vessels by both the government and their own communities.

When Theresa May was Home Secretary, she championed Muslim women's groups to specifically highlight women as incubators of Prevent within communities and families. In early 2016, the then-UK Prime Minister David Cameron introduced ESOL classes for Muslim mothers to fulfil his counter-extremism agenda, after cutting funding for these same classes previously.

Using the language of 'women's empowerment' to push Prevent has helped discredit and roll back such conversations and initiatives within Muslim communities and has fermented a culture of anxiety, undermined trust and created suspicion around any discussions relating to women's rights.

But it's worth reiterating that Muslim women exist both as part of Muslim communities and independently as human beings worthy of the same treatment and respect as Muslim men, and we cannot afford to hold off conversations simply for the sake of 'protecting' our communities. It is clearly specified in the Qur'an that we should be ready to speak for justice, even if it is against ourselves. We should never forego the high standards we have been set as Muslims for the sake of external actors' beliefs and behaviours.

Abuse and harassment remain pervasive; many Muslim women from a variety of ethnic backgrounds are reluctant to speak out about abuse because of the associated notions of shame and stigma. The recent #MosqueMeToo hashtag brought this conversation to the centre stage. However, our experiences are, yet again, being used as proxy battlefields for those who seek to use us to give into orientalist depictions of Muslim men as innately predatory, and those who wish for us to stay silent so as not to 'embarrass' Muslims and Islam itself.

This is perhaps a good time to point out that criticising cultural practices within Muslim communities, particularly the actions of Muslim men, doesn't equate to criticism of Islam and any attempt to argue otherwise is disingenuous at best.

Indeed, it is somewhat odd that there is a willingness from Muslim men to recognise and speak out against the violence experienced by Muslim women when it is at the hands of 'non-Muslims', but there is a blind-spot when it is Muslim men who are perpetuating that cycle of violence.

Reading about the recently surfaced allegations of international charities and their role in allowing the exploitation of Iraqi and Syrian women in conflict zones, the systematic rape and genocide of Rohingya women – these stories rightly incense us. Unfortunately, in the domestic sense, allegations surrounding abuse of power aren't as readily accepted. Yet another example of this is the murder of Samia Shahid. The publicity around the case has invited death threats and abuse towards prominent Muslim women who spoke out against the misogyny and controlling behaviour that ultimately led to her murder. Attempts to create honest and meaningful exchange around misogynist behaviours within our communities is met with immediate defensiveness and a lack of acceptance.

The manifestation of misogyny is all around us: from 'respectability' politics and the way women who don't conform to expectations of modesty or outward religiosity are demeaned, to the lack of adequate prayer spaces and female scholarship, to everyday experiences of harassment. We are locked in a struggle where women are at the forefront of the attacks that Muslim communities face; gendered Islamophobia, divide and conquer tactics, misrepresentation in the media, economic deprivation and assaults on civil liberties. We must remain at the forefront of challenging these too, but this can't be done without Muslim men, and it certainly can't be done unless we're able to challenge misogyny in all its forms and guises.

SAMAYYA AFZAL

Samayya Afzal is an activist based in Bradford, with experience in the higher education sector. She has held a series of elected student union positions, including the National Executive Council of the National Union of Students. She has also worked in diversity development, curating exhibitions related to the South Asian diaspora. Samayya currently works at the Muslim Council of Britain as Community Engagement Manager.

HAREEM GHANI

Hareem Ghani is a History undergraduate with an interest in feminist politics, race and religion. She was recently re-elected as Women's Officer for the National Union of Students (NUS), and spends her days organising and developing resources on harassment in Higher Education and Further Education.

Integration on Campus

There are over 329,000 Muslim students studying in the UK higher education system. They are spread across every subject area and corner of the country. Despite this fact, there are many issues and barriers for both UK and non-UK Muslims who choose to take up higher education studies.

For international Muslim students (this includes those who have come from within and outside of Europe), the heightened xenophobia that has been growing particularly in recent years, has left many feeling isolated and directly targeted. Immigration targets have been a key focus of this government, which has led to the deportation of countless international students, even prior to completing their studies and despite paying a large quantity of money to be able to do so.

International Muslim students already carry the huge weight of needing to succeed given the many sacrifices that their families and communities back home are likely to have made for them to come and study in the UK, but the added knowledge that they are in the most vulnerable position in this country has left many suffering from depression and anxiety with increasing number of suicides.

Furthermore, given the government's counter-terrorism strategy, many international students feel a constant policing of their every move and contribution in class. There is a fear of engagement in student union life as well as political spaces, because of the ways in which this policy targets activists, particularly those who are racialised and Muslim. Their precarious status in the country is exploited by universities as they will be warned that any involvement in demonstrations or political campaigns could jeopardize their right to be in the country.

During a national strike called by the Universities Colleges Union (UCU) many international Muslim students were in despair because they did not want to cross the picket lines — in opposition to the government's continued privatisation of education and the stripping of fair pay and pensions to lecturers and staff — but were told that they will be reprimanded for their solidarity and stripped of their visas.

> ### For all Muslim students, given that most come from communities of colour, there is a sense of growing oppression within the UK education system.

Both on a policy and societal level, Muslim international students feel unwanted. The racist depictions of Muslims in the media is heightened when it relates to those who are migrants. And some feel that Muslims who are UK nationals — at times — also internalise divisions that play into the good-Muslim bad-Muslim dichotomy that renders migrant Muslims as barbaric, uncivilised and innately violent.

For all Muslim students, given that most come from communities of colour, there is a sense of growing oppression within the UK education system. Many share experiences of micro-aggressions in classes from staff and fellow students — particularly felt in spaces where subjects refer to foreign policy, Muslim countries abroad or counter-terrorism i.e. International Relations, Politics and Sociology.

Even just walking across campuses, there have been a number of incidents of abuse hurled towards Muslim students and in some cases Islamophobic graffiti found on the walls. There is a sense of distrust towards the institutions to take adequate actions because the Prevent agenda is thought to be an institutionalised Islamophobia that the university complies with and therefore the belief that they are complicit in their discrimination. This is reinforced when Muslim students have chosen to take part in local student union elections and have experienced a huge Islamophobic backlash and attempts of character assassination and yet the institution often remains quiet.

Often the Islamic Societies within the students' unions are seen to be safe spaces where Muslim students can go for support, when they feel lonely and are suffering from mental health issues and even when they experience discrimination (because they don't trust the other services that exist). The fact that the Prevent agenda targets such spaces by even introducing cameras inside prayer rooms and swipe-card systems to monitor those accessing the space, means that the small sanctuary that some find in their Islamic Societies is being violated through this policy. Even on-campus counsellors are being forced to undergo Prevent training and provide the names of their patients who they feel are vulnerable, or susceptible to radicalisation. As one can imagine, many Muslim students have to think twice before accessing — at times — much needed help and support.

Recommendations
- Legal support and aid for international students facing deportations or unfair treatment/victimization during their studies.

- Support for Muslim political activists experiencing Islamophobic campaigns against them including media training and help, psychological support and potentially legal representation.

- Financial aid for Muslim students who seek mental health support.

MALIA BOUATTIA

Malia Bouattia is an activist and the former President of the National Union of Students who was the first Muslim and woman of colour elected into the post. She also co-founded the Students not Suspects campaign and writes for *The New Arab*, *Aljazeera*, the *Guardian*, *Huffington Post* and The *Middle East Eye*.

Getting the Best Out Of Young People

There has been much talk — and even a Channel 4 documentary — in recent years, trying to figure out 'What British Muslims want'. More often than not, these documentaries, articles and reports come to similar, generic conclusions. At worst, they treat British Muslims as a monolith while, at best, recognise only minor variations between Muslims living in Britain, directed by sect or ethnic background.

These analyses tend to downplay, if not disregard, how the identities of Muslims living in Britain today have changed and developed across generations — influenced not only by non-theological elements (i.e. foreign and domestic policy settings) but also the intersectional challenges that young Muslims face in an economy where it's even more difficult to attain a stable career, get on the housing ladder or even manage the debts that come with pursuing higher education.

There has been some advancement in conversation when speaking about the experiences and needs of young Muslims living in Britain today. Last year, photographer Mahtab Hussain released 'You Get Me?', a portrait series of young men living in one of Birmingham's most Muslim areas. The series illustrated the more complicated identities and challenges of the area's young Muslim men, which Hussain referred to in the *Financial Times* as an illustration of a 'crisis of masculinity'. In the series, Hussain's subjects talk about navigating their identities not only as Muslims, but as the sons of poor immigrant families, living in communities where there were few job opportunities and where local facilities like libraries and youth centres had left them little to be proud of. At the same time, these young men were confronted with their religious identity on a daily basis — but not on their terms. 'Some of the men spoke about experiencing discrimination' Hussain writes. 'They were repeatedly stopped and searched, labelled as a terrorist or an extremist and told that England wasn't their home. They were told to take on British values. But when they returned to their homeland, they were told they didn't belong there either. They were caught between two worlds.'

> ## *I have spoken to young men who say that preconceptions about their religious identity has meant they found it difficult to get jobs they wanted*

This conflict of identity has been repeated to me in various forms in the course of writing my upcoming book on Muslim identity in Britain with Hurst (2019). I have spoken to young men who say that preconceptions about their religious identity has meant they found it difficult to get jobs they wanted, or to pursue careers they had dreamt of in spaces largely dominated by white middle class people. Others, who have found career stability, told me they face similar issues when it comes to workplace discrimination based on preconceptions about Islam. 'I was called an extremist several times by my managers when I first started working,' one of my interviewees told me. 'They always told me they were joking — and that it was all part of workplace banter. But even as a Muslim who doesn't practice much, it affected me deeply'. For this interviewee, and plenty of others, the concept of a 'Muslim' goes beyond the religious or the theological. Its place in today's discourse is identitarian and occupies social, political as well as religious connotations.

This is particularly evident from the experiences of many young, visible Muslim women living in Britain, as recent reports from Faith Matters, the Young Foundation and others have shown. Last year, research commissioned by the government's social mobility watchdog showed that Muslim women from poorer backgrounds were the most discriminated against group of people in the UK when it came to accessing higher education or full time employment.

Despite this research, little seems to have changed in regards to government action. In addition to challenges Muslim women face when navigating spaces designed to allow for social mobility, Muslim women — particularly those who wear headscarves or niqabs, 'bear the brunt' of verbal and physical Islamophobic attacks in the UK according to a report published last year from TELL MAMA. The report showed that Muslim women made up 56% of all attacks recorded by police forces in the country — a number which is likely to be higher, considering that a large number of these attacks go unreported or do not fit into the frameworks set out by police forces when it comes to anti-Muslim abuse.

Even though successive government ministers and departments have been aware of these challenges, large swathes of Muslim communities generally feel that little has been done to tackle the problems Muslim in the UK face, and that policy setting toward Muslim communities has done little to represent Muslims at a time when a British-born generation is coming of age.

It is worth recognising that no single policy prescription, or umbrella strategy, will be sufficient to tackle all the problems that Muslim communities face. At the same time, it is worth recognising:

- British Muslims are not a monolith. Their differences are not simply theological or cultural. Generational differences between first, second and third generation Muslims mean that the priorities of communities change too.

- Young British Muslims face the same barriers as other young people living in the UK, in terms of getting jobs, access to education and entering the housing market. They should be more widely included in these conversations on a national level.

- Policymaking should recognise differences in the economic wellbeing in Muslim communities to form more nuanced strategies. Younger, poorer Muslim women face the biggest economic barriers across almost all areas of social mobility compared to better off Muslim men, so a single policy cannot address these inequalities.

- Young Muslims should be encouraged to participate in wider national conversations in a way that isn't directly in relation to their religious identities. They should be encouraged to participate in local and national political activism, volunteering, mentoring and creative schemes: not only to prepare them with skills for the future, but to actively foster a civic community for future generations of British Muslims.

Any new policy strategy will have to recognise the generational differences of young Muslims born and bred in the UK, and recognise the economic and social differences between communities: those who live in wealthy metropolitan cities and those who live in dilapidating industrial towns; those who are socially mobile with access to great schools and public facilities; and those whose public services have been cut and infrastructure projects scrapped as a result of austerity. Indeed, an umbrella strategy such as the current iterations of Prevent have done much to alienate many Muslim communities — many of whom are not reluctant to support a counter-terrorism policy, but rather recognising that the current policy does little to help vulnerable young people who face challenges similar to non-Muslim communities living in environments affected by poverty and little opportunity.

In this sense, 'What do Muslims want?' isn't necessarily the right question to ask. Rather, anyone interested in affecting change should ask how current policy around funding for local communities can help communities with large Muslim populations, how wider strategies around social cohesion can utilise young, active Muslims who are proud of their British identities. Perhaps, then, we will find that the needs and wants of young British Muslims aren't that different from other young, alienated people across the country.

HUSSEIN KESVANI

Hussein Kesvani is a journalist and writer based in London, UK. He is the UK & Europe editor of MEL magazine, and was previously a reporter at BuzzFeed UK, reporting on British Muslim affairs. He is currently writing his first book, on *British Muslim identity and the Internet*, for Hurst publishers (2019).

South London's Nigerian Community

Amongst many of the world's Muslims represented in our capital city, South London is home to many British Nigerians.

If 'Integration' is how people of different social backgrounds, generations, faiths, and ethnicities interact and build meaningful relationships, then, the fundamental basis of forming Coordinating Committee of Nigerian Muslim Organisations (CCNMO) was Integration.

After almost 4 years of consultation and negotiation, it was formally inaugurated on 26th October 1997. After a successful completion of the integration process, the organisation was restructured in October 2000 to become the Council of Nigerian Muslim Organisations (CNMO). As an umbrella body, the organisation was able to coordinate the activities of its members and sought to foster unity and cooperation among the organisations.

Because of this successful integration, the Nigerian Muslim community in the UK had now provided a forum for the imams of member-organisations to hold seminars, conferences and workshops on topical Islamic issues. This was done with the view to raising the level and quality of their religious and pastoral services to members of their respective organisations and the Nigerian Muslim community in the UK in general.

The CNMO believes in integration; it has achieved close and seamless coordination between several organisations by becoming a member of both local and national organisations, like Southwark Muslim Forum and the Muslim Council of Britain respectively. CNMO in its efforts to encourage integration among Muslims and other faiths, has been supporting its members to join its local and national interfaith group to widen integration.

This integration experience has filtered down from each member organisation to their respective individual members.

Social integration is a dynamic and structured process in which all members participate in dialogue to achieve and maintain peaceful social relationships of coexistence, collaboration and cohesion. The level of integration is usually measured through social networks, language, and intermarriage.

We have Nigerians in the UK who have contributed enormously to the development of Great Britain

In terms of social networks, Nigerian Muslim communities in the UK are mainly made up of Hausas from Northern Nigeria and Yorubas from Southern Nigeria. The majority are Yorubas, followed by Hausas and Igbo; even though we are from different backgrounds, Islam brought us together as one, and our official language is English as historically it was one of the British colonies. The Nigerians have established Islamic groups with regular congregations, as well as social gatherings for marriages, naming ceremonies and house warming ceremonies. We have Nigerians in the UK who have contributed enormously to the development of Great Britain in their varied career paths as politicians, doctors, engineers, lawyers, economists, accountants and entrepreneurs. Many have been recognised and have received honours from the Queen.

Language is another important variable to consider when assessing the degree of immigrants' social integration. Most Nigerians living in the UK will primarily speak the English language with their mother tongue used mostly in their native country. Nigerians communicate easily with local people and have been able to develop a better understanding of British culture, improving their access to the opportunities, rights and services available to mainstream society with cultural institutions such as mosques, churches and civic organisations.

Intermarriage is another indicator of social integration. The older generation of Nigerians are not as comfortable as the youth on intermarriage. The youth are more liberal when it comes to intermarriage and we can see practical examples among those of them who have chosen to marry non-Nigerians. There are a vast number of successful mixed-race people of Nigerian and British backgrounds that adore both heritages in our community.

Historically, Nigerians have been coming to the UK, mainly as students, ever since becoming a British Protectorate in 1914 and later gained independence in 1960 as a federation of three regions (Northern, Western, and Eastern). After their studies, some of them decided to engage in employment and even get married with both fellow Nigerians and White British. Many have children in the UK and see the UK at large as a second home.

Nigerian Muslims are not immune and have their own share of hatred, Islamophobia, and other incidents of discrimination affecting Muslims in general.

To make people integrate better in their community and into British society at large, more can be done by:

• Encouraging regular joint local educative events including celebrating ethnic minorities' successful contributions to the community. This should be organised by everyone from all ethnic backgrounds in the neighbourhood.

• Welcoming new neighbours warmly by existing local residents irrespective of ethnicity; being more tolerant and valuing each other's culture, language etc.

• Getting into the habit of caring for each other in the community by exchanging gifts, greetings and befriending them.

MAROOF ADEOYE

Maroof Adeoye is a social entrepreneur and a long standing consultant. He was a member of the Muslim Council of Britain's inaugural Central Working Committee nominated by National and Regional Organisations in 1997 and served for two terms as a delegate from the Council of Nigerian Muslim Organisations in the UK (CNMO) of which he is a founding Secretary General.

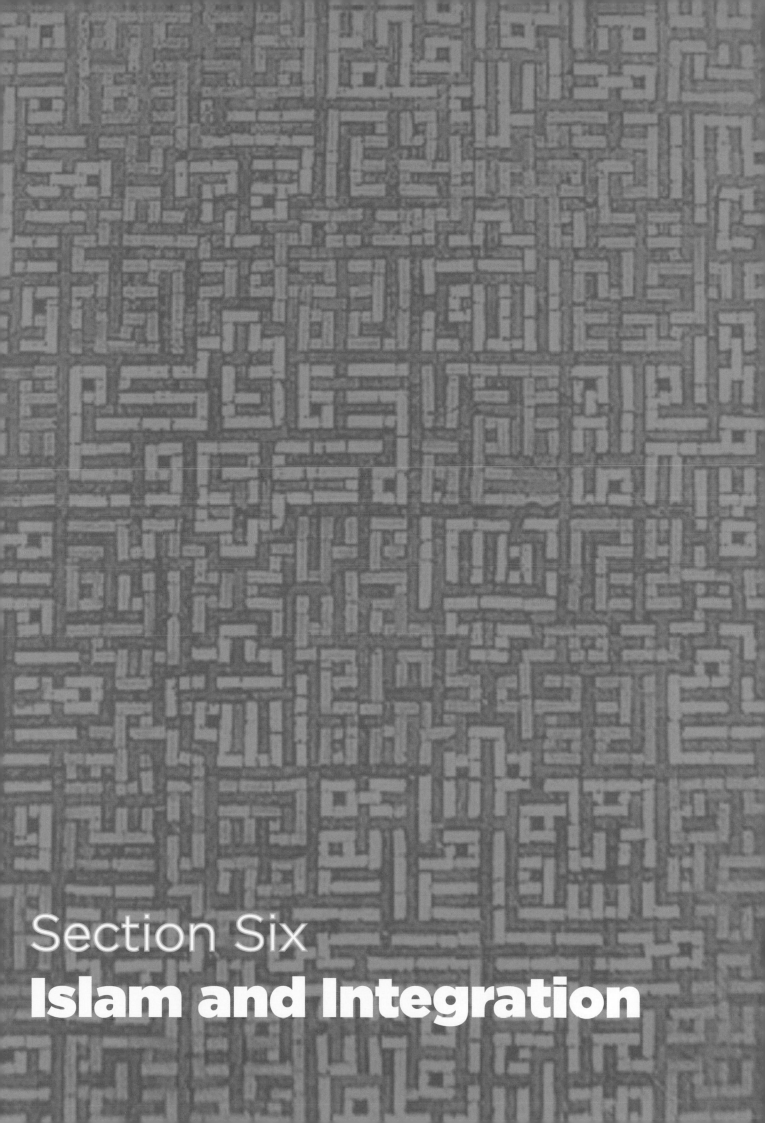

Section Six
Islam and Integration

Faith Helps Us Live in a Pluralist Society

At the heart of a Muslim's relationship to God is their relationship with other humans.

The cosmological order in Islam intimately connects Muslims and their spirituality to others, to nature and to God, each believer aspiring to emulate the beautiful names of God through their service to others, 'Be thou kind and good even as God has been good to thee.' (Qur'an 28:77) Harmony and goodness form the basis of the conduct of a Muslim, who is encouraged to strive not for temporal glory in this life but for virtuous character and good deeds that manifest in an eternal state of bliss, 'We grant the home in the Hereafter to those who do not seek superiority on the earth or spread destruction and disorder; the happy ending is awarded to those who are virtuous.' (Qur'an 23:83)

The concept of a 'community' that is served by Muslims, thus extends beyond the Muslim community itself, and draws no distinctions on the basis of faith, race, gender or social class. The unity is one centred on a shared humanity that acknowledges our deep set need for knowing one another, 'People, be mindful of your Lord, who created you from a single man and a single woman, and made you into nations and tribes, that you may know one another. Surely, the noblest among you in the sight of God are the most virtuous.' (Qur'an 49:13)

Within this concept of community, a special status is afforded to the weak, elderly and those in need; care and attention to them being prioritised so that they are shown generosity and kindness. The journey of a Muslim is experienced then not as an individual one, but one which carries a collective sense of consciousness and responsibility of contributing and doing good at the community and societal level.

For Muslims in the UK, such faith values, far from endorsing an insular existence, only reinforce an active commitment to being positive contributors to society. Moderated by introspection and a constant striving for perfecting the inner self, service to God is realised through acts of worship as well as service to society. Nature, family, neighbours and especially strangers all have a right over a Muslim's time, good actions, knowledge and wealth.

Central to the flourishing of communities embodying such values is the necessary inclusion of all members of society. Contrary to popular understanding, Islam does not segregate men and women, nor does it prioritise the participation and contributions of one over the other. In its rich history, Islam has facilitated the participation of diverse members across societies, notably women, who excelled across a broad spectrum of fields, especially scholarship. *Al-Muhaddithat*, a biographical encyclopaedia, re-illuminates a lost history of over 9000 biographies of Muslim female scholars who were active teachers and leaders throughout the history of Islam.

Muslim faith values offer additional richness to our understanding of what it means to live in a pluralist society and how to cultivate a space where individuals and communities can come together to fulfil their potential and work towards the common good.

AALIMAH ARZOO AHMED

Aalimah Arzoo Ahmed is Director at the Centre for Islam and Medicine, where she works with scholars and practitioners to explore the interaction of science, religion and ethics. Arzoo read Physics at the University of Oxford, after which she completed an MPhil in Medieval Arabic Thought at the Oriental Institute. She has an Alimiyyah degree in traditional Islamic studies, under the supervision of Shaykh Akram Nadwi, and is managing the publication of *Al-Muhaddithat*: a 40-volume encyclopedia on the history of Muslim female scholars.

Islam Does Not Sanction Segregation

Islam encourages and requires Muslims to integrate into the society which they have made their home. The diversity of race, culture, language and religion or the absence of it, is all part of God's plan and design. God tells us, '... For every one of you, We have appointed a right way and an open road. If God willed, He would have made you one single community, but (He has made you diverse) that He may test you in what He has given you. So compete with each other in good works. To God is your return, all of you together, and He will inform you about the things in which you differed.' (Qur'an 5:48). He also reminds us of our common and shared origins, 'O people, We have created you from a male and a female and We have made you into communities and tribes so that you may interact with one another. Indeed the most noble of you in God's eyes is the most righteous of you. Indeed God is All Knowing, All Aware.' (Qur'an 49:13).

Monasticism, total seclusion from worldly matters, isolating oneself from society and ghettoisation are forbidden in Islam. The Messenger Muhammad (peace be upon him) declared, 'There is no monasticism in Islam.' When his companions travelled to live with other communities he encouraged them to learn their language so that they could communicate and integrate with them and also be able to share their faith with their new neighbours. Muhammad himself went about his daily business like everybody else and into the hustle and bustle of the market place, something for which his detractors criticised him, 'And they said, 'What is with this Messenger? He eats food and walks in the markets. Why was an angel not sent down to him so that he could be a warner alongside him?' (Qur'an 25:7).

Muhammad taught that the best of people are those who are most beneficial to others. If one were to remain within a very closed and inward looking community then they would be drastically limiting their potential to benefit others. By integrating themselves in society, Muslims can be productive members of their communities

making vital contributions to the socio-economic development of society and offering an alternative lifestyle, which focuses not only on material wellbeing but critically also on spiritual wellbeing. History bears testimony to the fact that whenever and wherever any group has integrated into wider society, life has flourished for all concerned and communities have prospered. This is also true for Muslims.

Life for a Muslim revolves around five areas: belief in God and the articles of faith (*imaniyat*), worship of God (*`ibadat*), financial dealings with others (*mu`amalat*), social interaction with others (*mu`asharat*) and having a moral, ethical and upright character (*akhlaqiyat*). It is noteworthy that only two of the five areas have a direct relevance to God and three have a direct relevance to fellow human beings. Thus one can conclude that Islam places a lot more emphasis on integration and human relationships than the worship of God itself.

SHAYKH IBRAHIM MOGRA

Shaykh Ibrahim Mogra has been at the forefront in deepening inter faith and community relations in the UK and around the world, serving in leadership positions in a number of bodies including the Muslim Council of Britain and the Christian Muslim Forum. He holds religious credentials from Darul Uloom Al-Arabiyyah Al-Islamiyyah, Bury, U.K. as well as advanced theological qualifications from the Al-Azhar University in Cairo.

Speak Out Against Injustice Everywhere

Demographically speaking, there are well over two million Muslims residing in our country. In Birmingham, Britain's second city, Muslims will cease to be a minority and are projected to become a majority population. They have established excellent educational, philanthropic, welfare, community and spiritual organisations. Many of these institutions are pioneers and have excelled in their achievements. This is compounded by the fact that the vast majority of Muslims in this country are hard-working, law abiding, tax giving and peace-loving citizens who also vote various political parties based on varied political persuasions.

One would wonder why such an important group of people in this country and so ostensibly integrated into mainstream British society are still heavily marginalised, discriminated against and most worryingly, consistently identified as a threat to anything from British values to liberal democratic principles. Clearly this does not add up and it begs the question, why?

A knee-jerk reactionary answer to this may be racism, institutional discrimination or islamophobia. There is a degree of truth in this and much research academic or otherwise would evidence this. For example, when the grooming issues were presented in the media, it was related with a particular emphasis on Pakistani Muslim men; thus establishing an association between ethnicity and crime.

However, there is much more to this than mere victimisation. Muslims also have a significant role to play in this very unusual pattern and trend. For example, despite the many aforementioned positives, Muslims still do not have enough active political participation, very few pressure groups and tend to neglect various social issues and environmental concerns. This lack of effective and active participation results in a vacuum of absence. When you have such vacuums, you cannot expect them to be always filled by friendly voices. So, active participation in society and culture is a necessary imperative, not only because it is a current and real need but also because the very nature of our Deen demands it.

The Role of Believers

Allah describes the role and responsibilities of the Muslim Community: "You are indeed the best community that has ever been brought forth for [the good of] mankind: you enjoin the doing of what is right (*ma'roof*) and forbid the doing of what is wrong (*munkar*), and you believe in God." (Quran 3:110)

It is clear that the primary objective of bringing forth this community of believers is, to encourage the good and forbid the evil, partake in everything that is of benefit to the human race and to do everything within one's means to prevent harm to society. The *ma'roof* (good) referred to in the verse is unconditional and includes everything that falls within its definition, where it includes faith (*iman*) itself it also refers to charitable causes, endeavours to rehabilitate offenders, actions to spread literacy and education, efforts to save the environment, actions to bring about equality and justice, works to eliminate discrimination.

They would all fall within the perimeters of ma'roof and every Muslim is duty bound to contribute to these efforts. The same can be said about the word *munkar*, it is inclusive of all the problems and vices that exist in society. *Munkar* includes injustice, inequality, poverty, immorality, indecency, manipulation, exploitation, hoarding, criminality, oppression, all forms of abuse, domestic violence, neglect. Every Muslim is commanded by God Almighty to partake in society and struggle against these problems and to help free people from these evils.

Partaking Without Discrimination or Prejudice

Having outlined the primary responsibility of Muslims within their communities, it is important to point out that this responsibility is to be fulfilled irrespective of the faith, race or gender of the people involved. We are duty bound to partake in initiatives of good without any discrimination. This is clear from the Prophetic example. When the non-Muslim tribal leaders of Makkah, having witnessed the injustice perpetrated by some of their own, pledged to support the oppressed, to stand against anyone who oppressed another in Makkah and ensure the oppressors were held to account, our beloved Prophet was at the forefront of this pledge and considered it so virtuous that many years later he remarked:

"I had indeed witnessed a pact in the house of Abdullah ibn Jud'an that was more beloved to me than a herd of red camels. If I were called to it now in the time of Islam, I would respond." (Baihaqi)

The Prophet instructed his followers, the Muslim Community, to be at the forefront and partake in such initiatives, This was a general instruction where the good in the cause was the focal point irrespective of who initiated the cause or whom it affected. Furthermore, the Constitution of Madinah developed by the Messenger of God shows the importance of a cohesive community where every citizen has a duty of care to others in the community. This duty extends to the whole society.

The Perils of Not Partaking

We are living in a time in which apathy is on the rise and people are generally concerned with things that will benefit them personally, and as long as personal goals are achieved, minimal attention is given to issues that affect wider society. The Holy Prophet of Islam has instructed the Muslim community to avoid this attitude and warned about the dangers of disengaging and neglecting the duty of encouraging the good and dissuading from what is evil:

"The example of the person abiding by Allah's order and restrictions in comparison to those who violate them is like the example of those persons who drew lots for their seats in a boat. Some of them got seats in the upper part, and the others in the lower. When the latter needed water, they had to go up to bring water (and that troubled the others), so they said, 'Let us make a hole in our share of the ship (and get water) saving those who are above us from troubling them.

So, if the people in the upper part left the others to do what they had suggested, all the people of the ship would be destroyed, but if they prevented them, both parties would be safe." (Bukhari)

It is therefore imperative for the Muslim Community to engage, to affect a positive change and to prevent all forms of harm to our society and the people around us.

The above hadith clearly shows that failure to engage would mean that one sinks with society, because everything does affect everyone.

Every Little Helps

At times we fail to engage because we feel that our actions will not have a far-reaching impact. This should not be our worry, and no matter how insignificant our engagement may seem to us, it could be the 'straw that breaks the camel's back', in a positive sense of course! What may seem insignificant to us may well be of great virtue and importance in the sight of God Almighty.

Abu Dharr said: "The Prophet told me: Do not think of any good action as insignificant, even if it is the act of meeting your brother with a smile." (Muslim)

We must break away from an attitude of despondency and hopelessness, do our little bit and leave the results in the Hands of The One beyond whom there is no power. May Allah enable us to contribute effectively in our communities and become the beacons of hope for all those around us.

SHAYKH FAZL E MOHAMMED

Shaykh Fazl e Mohammed studied Islamic sciences at Jamia Al Karam and completed the Dars-e-Nizami at Dar al-Uloom Qadria Jilania, London. He undertook hadith studies at Dar al-Uloom Jamia Hanafia Sialkot, Pakistan. Currently he is the Head of Faith and Pastoral Care at HMP Nottingham and delivers classes on Islamic studies across the country.

The Importance of Relating to Others

Is Islam a stranger in the West in general or in British society in particular? What understanding should Muslims have of Islam and themselves here? What should others think about Islam and Muslims?

To answer the above questions adequately we need to first reflect on the nature of divine religions in general and Islam in particular. Divine messages are always universal. We cannot think that the God of everyone would discriminate in His message by addressing some and excluding others. This is not the way that God can be understood. No kind teacher or doctor would deprive some people from a good thing that he has to offer. In the same way, any message which comes from God is for everyone. Indeed, we can go further and claim that everything that belongs to God is for all. For example, the Ka'ba in Mecca which is known as the House of God, the Qur'an says: 'This is the very first house which is built for mankind' (3:96). The house of God is also the house of men, not the house of elites nor the house of some people. Anything that belongs to God is for everyone.

A message may start from one place and spread; just like light can emanate from one place and project itself, illuminating its surroundings. No one can say this light is only for us. Islam is for all, as the Prophet was also sent as a 'mercy for all people' (Qur'an 21:107). Muslims are not only supposed to benefit other Muslims; rather they are brought forth for the benefit of all people (Qur'an 3:110). Islam started in Mecca and then expanded into the Arab peninsula, but it was never meant to be only for Meccans or Arabs or only for the Middle East. Before the Prophet passed away, he offered the message to people of other empires and nations, including the kings of Iran and Yemen and the Emperor of Rome. Thus, the message is universal.

At the time of the Prophet, the message did not reach everyone. It spread slowly to other people. Generally, when the message is reaching out, it takes the form and shape of the people who have already embraced it. Islam is not an exception to this. To understand this better, we can look at the example of water which comes from rain and is pure but depending on the river bed, it can take different tastes. If it is a salty desert, the same water becomes salty and impossible to drink. Societies passed on the text of the Qur'an and Sunnah of the Prophet but with their own understanding, rituals, cultures and customs. For example, it may look more Arabic or Persian or Asian than merely Islamic. This may be also the case for parts of Christianity to the extent that some people forget that Christianity also started in the Middle East and Jesus was from Palestine.

One of the problems faced by the message is culturalisation. There is nothing wrong with cultures. Indeed, cultures play a great role in enriching and maintaining people's experiences of their religion. People can use their cultures and talents to give different, colourful presentations of the reality but they should not let these secretly replace the whole or parts of the message. For instance, you can bring food in any container but the container should not become so important that it diverts people's attention from the food or changes the taste or benefits of the food.

Unfortunately, many times the way cultures or traditions or religious communities have tried to establish identity in their adherents was by distancing themselves from others. So instead of saying what you are, the focus was on what you are not. And this is problematic. This is a type of identity which is based on fear and exclusion. And certainly, this type of understanding is neither compatible with Islam nor able to work in the world that we live in today. If it has worked in the past, it is because the world was very divided and partitioned. You could live in a town or even a country in which there were no people of other faiths, ethnicities or cultures. This is not the world today. And this type of fragile understanding of identity is not going to work today, and definitely not in the future.

We need to have a different type of understanding based on what you have and what you can offer to other human beings, and in turn appreciate what they have. Being able to relate to other people is an essential part of every person's identity today. I cannot be a good Muslim or Christian especially today, unless I know how to relate to other people and how to accommodate them in my own identity. And certainly, for believers in God, this is also a very important part of our faith. How can we believe in God, the Creator of all mankind, and then fail to care for part of the creation of God?

For us, not only does every human being carry the sign of God, but also every animal, every bird, every insect, every flower, every drop of water is significant because it is a manifestation of God.

So now, we need to rethink our understanding of our identity. If we look at a human body, we have different organs and different parts. Every organ has some function hence every organ has some identity. But if their understanding of their role is to exclude others or to ban others, then we are not going to survive. You can be an eye, you can be an ear, you can be a heart, but you can only survive if you understand how to relate to others and define yourself in a bigger unity.

This type of understanding is what we need. And when I look at the Qur'an, I see that this is actually the plan of God. God has made lots of arrangements in His creation and legislation so that we would move towards unity. I think what would help communities to develop a new sense of their identity and facilitate the process of opening up themselves to a wider unity, is to give them reassurance that there is no attempt to pressurise them to assimilate or to eliminate their identity or marginalise them. When cultures, traditions and religious communities feel more comfortable and safe, they open up more and become more hospitable and more respectful of each other.

SHAYKH MOHAMMAD ALI SHOMALI

Shaykh Mohammad Ali Shomali is a graduate of the Islamic Seminaries of Qum. He earned his Doctorate in Philosophy from the University of Manchester, and did his postdoctoral research on ethical issues related to life and death. He is involved in interreligious dialogue and has presented papers on this topic across the world.

Will I Always Be An Outsider?

Will I always be an outsider, considered 'taken in'
A favour to my ancestors, because of the colour of
my skin?
Will the state always need to target a minority
Just to shore up its own fragile authority?
Will Bob who lost his job because of advancing
technology
Still blame my brother and expect an apology?
Still blame my mother for rising inequality?
Still look for a scapegoat and an easy ideology
That tells him that the problem is from those who
migrate
Who simultaneously take jobs yet won't 'integrate'?
See, he doesn't have a problem with those that look
like him
Those that dress like him, it's only if you're Muslim
That there's a problem, and either you must change
Drop your cultural baggage and start to arrange
Your life according to certain standards & positions
Certain norms and conditions
Because anyway it's a backward religion
That needs an 'enlightenment' or modern transition
And if you disagree, then you can go back 'home'
Even though this country is all you've ever known.

I've been told many times that I must 'integrate'
It seems to make it easier for someone else to relate
So the focus is shifted and the burden is on me
To justify my own humanity.
So forgive me if I challenge the central assumption
That somehow I'm responsible for societal
dysfunction
That somehow I should just 'integrate' more

So the attention is on me, not on foreign policy and
war
Not on funding cuts that deprive entire
communities
Not on austerity and how it drives disunity
Not on unequal applications of terrorism legislation
So you're really only charged if you're black or
Asian.

And if despite all this, you continue to insist
I must 'integrate', as though all I do is resist
Then please answer me this
How many Muslims exist
Working in our emergency services
In hospitals and surgeries as doctors and nurses?
How much do Muslims donate each year?
How many of us are there, in the public sphere?
How many more Mo Farahs will it take
Before we can finally put an end to this debate?
We shouldn't have to prove our worth to this nation
When most of us are only here because of
colonisation.
So isn't it time we moved on the conversation?
And took 'integration' out of the equation?
Because ultimately in a world that's been artificially
divided
By lines on a map elsewhere decided,
All of us are just trying to improve our situation
Find a better life for ourselves and the next
generation
Surely that's not something so controversial
But an accepted truth, a value universal.

NARJIS KHAN

Narjis Khan is a practising solicitor with degrees from Cambridge University and the LSE. She began writing poetry in 2016 on topics including racism, Islamophobia and immigration.

CASE STUDY:

Visit My Mosque

What is #VisitMyMosque?

#VisitMyMosque day is a national initiative facilitated by the Muslim Council of Britain (MCB), encouraging mosques across the UK to hold mosque open days. It aims to dispel myths and misconceptions about Muslims and Islam by facilitating conversations and dialogue between Muslims and their local neighbours of all faiths and none.

Most recently on 18th February 2018, over 200 mosques across England, Scotland, Wales and Northern Ireland welcomed in thousands of Britons for the fourth consecutive #VisitMyMosque day.

The initiative saw some of the country's oldest mosques open their doors including the Abdullah Quilliam Mosque in Liverpool, the first mosque in the UK established in 1887, as well as the Shah Jahan Mosque in Woking, the UK's first purpose-built mosque established in 1889.

Some of the UK's most remote cities also took part, including mosques in Inverness, Cornwall, Hastings and Ipswich, as well as larger mosques in major cities such as East London Mosque, Birmingham Central Mosque, Leeds Grand Mosque, Glasgow Central Mosque and Cardiff's Dar Ul-Isra.

Since the initiative's inception in 2015 it has grown in popularity, from 20 mosques in the first year, to 80, then 150 and now over 200 mosques in 2018. The theme for 2018 was "Open Doors, Open Mosques, Open Communities."

Long Term Relationships

Following the mosque open day, mosque leaders and visitors are encouraged to exchange contact details and organise further outreach events together, including mutual visits to churches, mandirs, synagogues, gurdwaras or other places of worship in the local area if possible, in order to develop long-term relationships with each other.

A YouGov poll commissioned by the Muslim Council of Britain revealed that almost 70% of Britons hadn't seen the inside of another faith's place of worship, and almost 90% hadn't been inside a mosque in the last five years. #VisitMyMosque seeks to address this by accelerating ongoing efforts for people of different or no faith to get to know each other, thereby increasing community cohesion.

Countering Islamophobia

With a steady stream of negative press primarily around terrorism, it may be understandable why some people might hesitate to set foot inside a mosque. Some may worry about what to do at mosques, whether women have equal access, or question certain practices in our faith.

These are all valid concerns, but the #VisitMyMosque initiative welcomes these conversations and hopes the great British public will use the opportunity to go and visit their local mosque and put these questions to their Muslim neighbours.

Social Hubs

While the five daily prayers are the central activity in mosques, other activities go hand-in-hand. They are the hub of the community and a place for social action. Visitors are often surprised to find their local mosque organising food drives and family fun days, soup kitchens for the homeless, fundraising for local causes and much more.

#VisitMyMosque day also hopes to tell the story of how mosques are very much part of the fabric of British society and positively contributing to their local areas.

What Next

#VisitMyMosque is planned to continue as an annual initiative with the next day organised for early 2019.

For more information visit www.visitmymosque.org or search #visitmymosque

Muslim Council of Britain

List of Contributors

HARUN KHAN
Secretary General,
Muslim Council of Britain

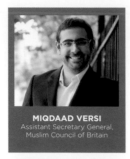

MIQDAAD VERSI
Assistant Secretary General,
Muslim Council of Britain

RT HON DIANE ABBOTT
Labour MP, Shadow Secretary
of State for Home Affairs

**RT HON DOMINIC GRIEVE
QC MP**
Conservative MP, Chair,
Intelligence and Security
Committee

**BARONESS SAYEEDA
WARSI**
Conservative member of the
House of Lords

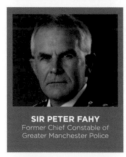

SIR PETER FAHY
Former Chief Constable of
Greater Manchester Police

**PROFESSOR JONATHAN
PORTES**
Professor of Economics and Public
Policy, King's College London

NAOMI GREEN
Belfast Islamic Centre

AMANDA MORRIS
Administrative Executive,
Muslim Council of Wales

ADREES SHARIF
Vice President, UK Islamic
Mission (Midland Zone)

FAZ PATEL MBE
Social Entrepreneur

SUFIA ALAM
Centre Manager, Maryam
Centre

SAMAYYA AFZAL
Community Engagement
Manager, Muslim Council of
Britain

**DR KHADIJAH
ELSHAYYAL**
Post-Doctoral Research Fellow,
University of Edinburgh

ESMAT JERAJ
Community Organiser, Sponsor
Refugees Foundation, Citzens
UK

HASHI MOHAMED
Junior Barrister, The
Honourable Society of Lincoln's
Inn

ANDY HULL
Councillor, Highbury West

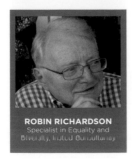

ROBIN RICHARDSON
Specialist in Equality and
Diversity, Insted Consultancy

SUE LUKES
Chartered Institute of Housing

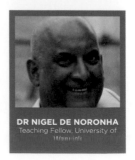

DR NIGEL DE NORONHA
Teaching Fellow, University of
Warwick

MAZ SALEEM
Anti-war and anti-racist
campaigner

FRANCES O'GRADY
General Secretary, Trades Union
Congress

NAIMA KHAN
Programme Manager, MFest

TUFYAL CHOUDHURY
Director, MFest

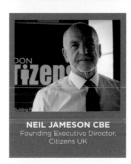

NEIL JAMESON CBE
Founding Executive Director,
Citizens UK

**DR MUHAMMAD ABDUL
BARI MBE**
Community Activist,
Educationalist

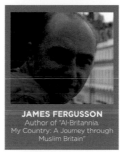

JAMES FERGUSSON
Author of "Al-Britannia.
My Country: A Journey through
Muslim Britain"

HAYYAN BHABHA
Executive Director,
MuslimsinWW1.com

MOHAMED-ZAIN DADA
Co-founder, Decolonising Our
Minds Society

BATOOL AL TOMA
Director, New Muslims Project

HAREEM GHANI
Women's Officer, National
Union of Students

MALIA BOUATTIA
Former President,
National Union of Students

HUSSEIN KESVANI
UK & Europe Editor, MEL
Magazine

MAROOF ADEOYE
Founding Secretary General,
Council of Nigerian Muslim
Organisations

AALIMAH ARZOO AHMED
Director,
Centre for Islam and Medicine

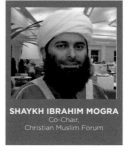

SHAYKH IBRAHIM MOGRA
Co-Chair,
Christian Muslim Forum

**SHAYKH FAZL E
MOHAMMED**
Head of Faith and Pastoral Care,
HMP Nottingham

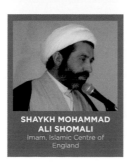

**SHAYKH MOHAMMAD
ALI SHOMALI**
Imam, Islamic Centre of
England

NARJIS KHAN
Cambridge University Graduate
and Practising Solicitor